DISCOVERING TREE MAGIC WITHIN

the magic of trees

JESSICA MARIE BAUMGARTNER

WITCH WAY
PUBLISHING

First Edition, 2023

Witch Way Publishing
3436 Magazine Street
#460
New Orleans, LA 70115
www.witchwaypublishing.com

Editor: Tonya A. Brown
Cover Designer: Quirky Circe Book Designs
Copy Editor: Anna Rowyn
Internal Design: Emily Barta & Tonya A. Brown
Illustrator: Leighanna Miller

Printed in the United States of America

ISBN Paperback: 978-1-08792-6872
ISBN E-Book: 978-1-08806-1039

To the forest spirits.

CONTENTS

INTRODUCTION

S WAYING BRANCHES, LEAFY CORNERS HIDING IN THE SHADE, emerald seas painting the sky: just visualizing a forest calms the human spirit. We breathe deeper, smile easier.

For centuries humans looked to trees as friends. They provide shelter, oxygen, and sometimes fruits, nuts, or saps. Their continuous place in our survival and that of the planet will never change. No matter how modern society shifts or ignores our direct connection to these rooted beings, they answer many of the questions we seek.

When searching for meaning, understanding, or acceptance, the boughs never mock or shame me. The roots remain consistent and supportive when working to better myself or maintain a balanced lifestyle.

From sapling to ancient towers of trunk and limbs, we all possess the ability to connect with trees on every level of existence. Our bodies benefit from walking among growth and vegetation. Our lungs heal from pollution when breathing in pure air. Our thoughts become clearer when we get away from dense radio and satellite signals pounding into major cities and across nations.

When an individual befriends all the life surrounding them, they walk an enchanted path. They become more perceptive. Messages drift on the wind. Bird song becomes more than a territorial call. The future unfolds with grace and dignity.

Peace is possible through tree magic. It is clear. It is untainted. There is no corruption in the wild world of the wooden giants.

Aging is revered when a being discovers what the trees already know. The old ones are looked upon with wonder and awe and can properly pass on their knowledge in an environment that does not shun death or nature's cycles. Fear is irrelevant in the person who practices the art of consecrating themselves and the trees through that great unchanging bond the universe has gifted us.

The spirit awakens to solutions and possibilities untouched when drawing on the magic held within the fibers of the world's most beautiful giants. Age-old truths become more apparent. All the power and energy a person has is refined when expanded through forestry.

Our links begin as we grow into existence. We are cultivated and brought into the world, ready to grow and find purpose. Childhood extends the roots of who we are, setting the limits we will have to reach beyond. Once fully developed, people must look beyond themselves to acknowledge the similarities between themselves and the trees.

Once achieved, it becomes essential to protect and preserve the beings that lumber together to produce forests of clean air and shelter. Planting becomes sacred.

Even sprouts produce parallels to our lives once adulthood is constant. Modernity, societal pressures, commerce, business, and competition often mask what empowers people with the strength needed to maintain a healthy aspect: nature, balance, and simple pleasures. But society is learning. Humans are intelligent and can adapt when accepting the necessity.

How cities and suburbs are built can be molded to nurture a world that desperately requires sustainability. Ecological additions can be implemented by housing developers. Tax breaks, grants, or public support can push corporations to plant more greenery around their buildings to support wildlife and clean living.

These efforts are more strongly felt within communities directly, and affect how families and individuals can improve their lives and that of the world around them. By offering more green spaces, children can grow and connect with nature without interference. As nurturers, parents, and caretakers stand before children like great oaks. They are often more apt to recognize their tree energies. Although adults are more versed in navigating the natural elements, young children are just as similar to growing trees. It is wise to explore that connection and encourage little ones to explore that energy with guidance and an appreciation for the great outdoors.

As adults, we tower over our young, leading by example. It is not always easy to make room for youth, but when facing the magic of ancient trees, a person is more apt to understand the entire landscape. We must recognize the importance of caring for the smallest of beings in order to make room for what is to come.

This attention to the needs of future generations drowns out fleeting excesses. It eases the mind and fine-tunes personal power for greater purposes.

The leaves of this book are categorized by different branches, but the trunk is sturdy. The roots are equal in knowledge and importance. I have worked to help them grow through my own course. There has been a severe disconnect from nature as the technological age has advanced. This had grown to the point that even just planting a tree or stopping to enjoy the beauty of a great pine has become less common.

However, these words touch the base of your being; I hope you can rediscover the tree energy within and allow that to redirect your actions toward a stronger relationship with the trees that give us life. Just as each breath is impossible without the trees, this book would not exist if it weren't for their love.

TREE MAGIC AND THE INNER CHILD

WHO WE ARE IS FORMED FROM BIRTH AND rooted in what we experience in childhood. It branches out from that base into adulthood and beyond. The inner child is the person inside of everyone who is unafraid to try new things, ask questions, and find joy in simplicity.

Even the tallest trees do not leave behind the original seed. Everything is reconstructed and used as fuel for growth. Balanced individuals are like that. A person cannot flourish if they remain immature, but they also need to balance childlike wonder to appreciate who they are and what is possible. No matter where one comes from or what one may have suffered, whimsy and joy are found in some aspect of life, even if it is escapism.

I often think back. What was my earliest happy memory? Why does it matter? How has it helped along the way?

Even the foggiest visions of playing with coasters on my grandparents' coffee table as a toddler give me insight into who I am and where I need to be. Just touching those wooden coasters helped me to learn and appreciate where the materials that made them came from and why trees are a resource that must continue to be respected throughout life. Beyond that, incorporating the simple lessons of youth into the more complex life of adulthood aids in connecting with a greater purpose. It draws out otherwise suppressed energies and often keeps things moving with a sense of humor.

The gods like to laugh. That's why life sometimes becomes absurd. In all its harshness, even nature holds playful moments where graceful creatures trip over themselves. It's all part of a balanced existence.

I must keep my sense of humor to try new things and start a new adventure. Understanding that the energies surrounding everyone host whimsical excursions are a start, but in truth, engaging in that lighthearted nature is what breeds courage. It takes bravery to face the unknown—especially when growing older.

As a child, fear is less defined. With each year, negative experiences, reports, and input have the power to stunt a person's growth before they even begin new journeys.

Determining to push past the naysayers or past grievances and reach for a greater purpose builds personal power. It breeds confidence and taps into the deeper instincts embedded in us from seed to birth. The need to explore, achieve, and master a new skill or endeavor is key to maintaining the link to one's inner child. Hanging on to the will to be curious requires flexibility and strength all at once.

Instead of standing firm with stubborn audacity, laughter grasps our spirit and allows us to more readily accept that we cannot control everything around us. This ability to flow with the winds as they shift and change opens us up to new ideas. It allows a person to ask questions without being disrespectful. Challenging common thought, the status quo, is not a simple task but can be approached based on the solid soil of common ground.

Relating to others while bringing valuable questions and concerns to light bonds those seeking true knowledge and wisdom. The great oaks of a community do not fear new ideas. In return, the inexperienced who wish to provide nutrients for all roots must appreciate the truths only lent to age and experience.

Looking up to others is a great way to balance the inner child with the deeper concerns of adulthood or coming of age. Finding the voices of those who are honorable and enriching their nutrients with a variety of information to form independent thought designs fertilizer for spiritual and intellectual growth.

Like the trees of a forest that rely on the strength of the oldest to guide new roots as they twist further beneath the surface, humans also require direction. Finding the inner compass is less complicated than one may think. Like a riddle that solves too easily, charging energies to keep the spirit young is less defined by great displays of ability and more magnified/attained through small joys.

Even the most enlightened beings smile at a flower. The strongest trees still bow to saplings when the wind blows. Their simple grace is akin to the bliss of childhood.

Drawing that flexibility forth opens internal pathways. It recalls ancient wisdom that hides in genetic memory and collective truths that remain a constant aspect of existence. To speak to the self's most innocent hopes and memories without societal, familial, or personal constraints takes a whimsical approach. And when that goal is attained, spiritual and mental ascension is possible.

Meditations offer more guidance for those who do not hide from who they are. Spells take on new meaning. Rituals blossom into life-long ceremonies. Discovering the future through the past becomes an adventurous process.

1

TREE MEDITATIONS
FOR
THE INNER CHILD

S A CHILD, MY FRIENDS AND I PRETENDED to be animals. We looked to these creatures for guidance and climbed trees, never realizing that the branches and limbs themselves were unlocking magic hiding beneath our hands. Over time the bond between bark and birth grew deeper. The picnics and games played before forest giants stayed with me.

The energies built and obtained in the forests guide everyone who listens without requiring profound lessons, rules, or judgments. A sense of love and enjoyment is built and tended.

Keeping hold of that power may seem difficult as time passes, but strengthening or recalling it is possible through meditation.

Whether visualizing or traipsing among the woods, there are methods for everyone.

Tree Shadow

(To be done when struggling to accept change or feeling out of balance)

Step 1: On a clear day, sit beneath a familiar tree with your back against the trunk.

Step 2: Look up to the branches reaching above. Watch the movements overhead. Whether wind, the changing position of the sun, or the movements of creatures, study the fluidity of existence. Think of how everything that lies before you is linked to your current situation.

Step 3: Now gaze around in front and to the sides of you. See how everything at eye level is alive with the surrounding elements. Visualize the essential aspects of life that nurture and encourage you to grow. Whether these are the bonds you share with a caring friend/family member, or the time spent reading useful information, these elements are necessary to your personal evolution.

Step 4: When ready, look down upon the ground. Study the shadows, the fallen sticks and twigs. Let the mosses or insects offer perspective in a world where humans are falsely seen as more important than other smaller creatures with just as much purpose. Open yourself to the endless future. Find the truth in the fact that no matter how high we reach, we will all meet our fall and become part of the shadows that return us to the earth and break down our physical form.

Step 5: Place 1 hand on the ground and hold the other up. Close eyes. Breathe in and out deep and slow. Focus on the tree and its shadow.

See how the fates are connected. Think of how our shadows are a simple representation of who we are on the outside, but also dark and mysterious, like the complex secrets we hide when feeling self-conscious.

Step 6: Now direct your attention to your own life. Switch hands, placing the one on the ground towards the sky and the one that was up on the ground. Keep your eyes closed and control your breathing. Let everything come together. Visualize your place in the grand scheme. Let that lead your mind to a greater purpose to become more self-aware. Think of what truly matters to you and what you wish to accomplish in the short and long term. Slowly work out how you can achieve this.

Step 7: Open your eyes and glance ahead, then down, then up. Smile at what you have seen and get up to walk further in the world.

Tree Breathing

(To be done when needed to clear your mind/connect to happier thoughts)

Step 1: Stand steady with your arms at your sides.

Step 2: Close your eyes and see yourself in a forest surrounded by trees.

Step 3: Breathe deep. Visualize your lungs filling and the oxygen expanding through your body, clearing the brain. Reach your arms up and sway.

Step 4: Breath out. Think of how each exhale supplies plants and greenery with fuel and how we rely on each other for survival. Bring arms back down to sides. »

Step 5: Repeat this process for as long as needed. Let each breath open up the senses with purpose. Allow the mind to examine new thoughts beyond.

Strengthening the Trunk

(To be done when feeling under pressure or in need of a pick-me-up)

Step 1: Take a nature walk or, if unable, wander around the backyard/familiar wooded area. Find a large fallen tree or stump to sit on.

Step 2: Simply rest on the stump with your legs firm on the ground and back straight, hands on knees.

Step 3: Think of the strength that once held the section of the tree you are sitting on. The layers and fibers came together to stand erect and use that energy.

Step 4: Visualize your spine as a tree. It must hold firm but also be flexible for moving and shifting. Hold the straight-up position breathing in and out for as long as possible.

Step 5: Then, sway. Gently. Don't slouch or lose form, but rock from side to side with head high and shoulders back like a great tree would move and dance with the wind. Let the body loosen while keeping its strength. Do at least 3 times for as long as necessary.

Step 6: Now lightly dip back, then pull forward while keeping the head high and shoulders back with the spine tucked and in control. Do it at least 3 times for as long as necessary.

Step 7: Regain the sitting position and keep still. Acknowledge any changes in the body or energy levels. Pat the tree or stump beneath you and thank it for providing a good base. Then go on your way.

Climbing the Sky

(To be done when looking to expand the mind or seek new ideas)

Step 1: Sit tall in a comfortable space and close your eyes.

Step 2: Clear the mind. Breathe deep. Focus on the sensation of your breathing and the heat it generates. Let that energy build and spread throughout your body.

Step 3: Cross your arms over your chest and visualize yourself as a tree. Imagine that your spine is a tree trunk, and your arms are the branches. Slowly bring them out as you inhale and exhale.

Step 4: Once your arms are fully extended, sway side to side at least 3 times, then rock backward and forward at least 3 times. With every breath, think of your arms as branches expanding, not just physically but emotionally—spiritually.

Step 5: Allow the heat within to power to grow and expand. As it matures, utilize it to focus on emotional and spiritual issues or concerns that have blocked you from reaching out to others or meeting your goals/needs.

Step 6: Hold your arms out until they burn. Feel the strain, the stress that is necessary to reach your full potential. Being strong and open is somewhat painful, but no achievement can be met without that pain.

Step 7: Stretch your arms and enjoy the relief. Consider anything brought to light and focus on looking beyond the short-term meaning. Ponder how your experience offers guidance for the future.

Upward Journey

(To be done when in need of solutions to new problems)

Step 1: Go to a sturdy tree that is familiar. Pines are often great for climbing (but also sticky).

Step 2: Stand at the trunk and gaze up. Look at the branches and imagine your hopes or most far-reaching goal. See each branch is an obstacle to the top that represents achievement.

Step 3: Find the best positioning to start and think of the easiest, most immediate obstacle as you climb that branch. Once you gain your footing and are stable, think of the next easiest immediate obstacle and conquer it through climbing.

Step 4: With each new branch, see different ways to tackle the real issue and plan a strategy to overcome it.

Step 5: Continue to climb as high up as possible. It is okay to not reach the top. This meditation can be repeated as often or as needed with different trees if necessary. It is not an exercise in conquering but a practice in discipline, logic, and persistence.

Step 6: Take the time to work at it and eventually reach the top of a tall tree. The energies bred in the branches will aid in all other areas of life. When reaching the top, go ahead and look down. It's important to see your hard work and where it's brought you.

Step 7: Climb back down, but on the way, instead of focusing on obstacles or the goal itself, think of friends or colleagues who would benefit from your aid. Think of ways to help them meet their goals or climb after their dreams.

Step 8: When stepping back on the ground, look up once more and smile at your success.

Listen to the Leaves

Step 1: Climb a familiar tree or gather fallen branches and/or leaves to place in a circle and sit in the center.

Step 2: Carefully grasp a different branch in each hand or visualize doing so. Breathe deep and feel your pulse meeting the tree/bark.

Step 3: Focus on the sensation of touch, and the air's energies. Is it humid? Is it cool? What does the wind feel like? Is there any at all today, and how does it affect you?

Step 4: Listen intently and keep the mind clear but centered on connecting with the tree and its leaves. Really focus on how the tree affects your mood and your spirit. Harsh gusts may blow and rustle many voices, or stillness may bring a clarifying silence. The main goal is to keep the mind clear and open to any new insights or spiritual revelations that may transpire. These can come quick as fleeting thoughts or become longer visualizations that follow you off the ground. Each experience is different but can aid your spirit.

Step 5: When all concentration has been exhausted, climb down/stand in the circle. Raise arms to the sky. Then reach down to the ground. Think of what revelations came or what ideas are sparked from this experience, and let them stay with you.

Following the Patterns

(To be done when wishing to better connect with nature)

Step 1: Bring paper and crayons along on a walk in the woods or around the home. Use these to take rubbings of the bark patterns of different trees. (At least 2)

Step 2: When finished, find a comfortable place to sit and meditate on those lines displayed in these tree rubbings.

Step 3: Gently slide your fingers over the first image. Visualize the tree it came from and the sensations that the rubbing inspires.

Step 4: Repeat this with the second, and so on, until you've gone through all of them.

Step 5: Place one hand on the first rubbing you did, and the other on the last one you did. Close your eyes and feel the images. Think of where they came from and the questions or thoughts they inspire. Follow that path through the mind and feel out the pattern's markings. The ideas remain within you.

Step 6: When you feel lightheaded or unable to concentrate any longer, roll the rubbing up, tie it with string, and bring them home to set aside for safe keeping or to burn during the next seasonal ritual.

Sap and Song

(To be done when needing courage)

Step 1: Walk among a familiar tree or wooded area.

Step 2: Breathe in the air and listen to the sounds around you. Acknowledge and appreciate bird calls, creaking limbs, rustling leaves, or the shaking grasses under squirrel feet.

Step 3: Go before the roots and get comfortable. Sit, stand, or kneel.

Step 4: Acknowledge the rhythm of nature. Really focus on it and think of the natural noises as music. Listen and let the sounds sing. Then add in your own melody. Unafraid and whimsical, blend your soft hum or a loud, bold phrase, and let the melody/words come easily without much thought. Refrain from clouding your mind trying to plan everything.

Step 5: Naturally breathe in the bark-scented air. Feel the energy your sounds create and laugh at the simplistic nature of the song. Enjoy the chills or rush of warmth that may follow. Revel in that childish ability to sing or hum anywhere you go.

Step 6: Reach out for the tree and feel its influence on the area. Let its great strength solidify the moment with a conscious knowledge that this experience is unique and fun. Then bow to the tree and become silent once more. Listen. Specific thoughts and messages may come to mind; Lend them some time.

Step 7: When ready to finish, pat the ground and go on your way.

Rooted Without Bounds

(To be done when feeling disconnected from yourself and/or the world)

THE WORK:

Step 1: Go before a familiar tree and kneel at its roots.

Step 2: Lean forward and press your ear to them.

Step 3: Rollover, lie on your back with your head upon the tree roots and gaze up at the branches. Visualize the roots growing as deep and wide as the limbs above. Don't be afraid to get down and dirty.

Step 4: Hold your arms up and gaze at them. Bend your knees and dig your feet into the ground.

Step 5: Feel how the blood rushes. Now sit up and focus on that gravitational pull.

Step 6: Stand up and place each foot on a root or as close as possible if no roots are unearthed. Look down and think of where your life began, how it is rooted in some ways and compressed in others.

Step 7: See the main childhood issue you wish to move away from. Think of how it has affected your growth and ability to feel adequately nurtured. Visualize this issue in the dirt. Now step back and turn away from it.

Step 8: Mentally see your path veering away from the issue and commit to a different direction.

Step 9: Bow to the ground and go on your way.

2

TREE RITUALS FOR
THE INNER CHILD

NCORPORATING TREES INTO RITUAL LIGHTENS THE ATMO-
SPHERE. SABBATHS and Full Moon Blessings do not have to be
dry, solemn occasions. I cannot take myself that seriously. Stone-
faced ideals hold no connection to the beauty of life that I know.
Laughter and love must radiate around me, or I feel disconnected
from the Rites I perform.

Keeping in touch with the inner child balances that. One can come
prepared with dedication while smiling and joking before the gods . The
following rituals were not written in a sober manner; they are second
nature to me. The trees and my playful sides come together to draw the
better aspects of who I am in the modern world.

Growing Magic

(To be done when seeking emotional growth)

MATERIALS NEEDED: Pen, paper, offering of food scraps, garden shovel, bonfire

PREPARATION: Collect food scraps/leftovers for at least 3 days until the ritual. Do it during the full moon.

THE WORK:

1. Sit before the bonfire with your offering and the shovel. Set them beside you, and write down your emotional needs that are not being met.

2. Turn the paper over and list what needs to be done by yourself and others to change this.

3. Meditate on the flames before you. Focus on how the issue can be remedied and your internal growth. Feel the warmth inside you spread and let it branch out.

4. Go before a nearby tree, and bring the offering, paper, and shovel along. Kneel at its roots.

5. Hold the paper before the food, set it on top of scraps, and dig a hole for the offering.

6. Once more, take up the paper and think over its meaning. Now fill the hole with your offering and place the paper on top.

7. Return the dirt to its rightful place and cover the offering and paper. While burying these items, whisper, sing, or chant to borrow the growing energies of the trees so you can expand your abilities and meet your emotional needs.

8. Set your shovel aside and press both palms on the fresh soil. Thank the tree and bow to it. Then continue with other full moon activities.

Dropping Games

(A spatial and internal cleansing)

MATERIALS NEEDED: Self, large fire stick/staff, matches
PREPARATION: Do on Samhain or Yule.

THE WORK:

1. On the day of the ritual, take a nature walk or walk around the yard and collect sticks and twigs. Take your time. Really stretch your limbs with each bundle.

2. Each time your arms get full, walk the bundle over to the fire pit or ritual fire area and place your sticks in a pile facing the same direction (these sticks will not be used to create and start your fire).

3. Keep building this pile up. (For those who are more creative, you can create patterns or images out of your stick piles).

4. When it is time to light the fires, choose a few twigs and sticks for kindling, but keep the main stack for the full blaze.

5. As the fires begin to burn, relax. Once it is time for spellwork and performing specific acts of magic, grasp a single stick and hold it up. Speak, chant, or sing of letting go of what has been to cleanse the self for what is to come. Then throw the stick into the fire.

6. If other members are partaking, have each do the same one by one.

7. Meditate on moving forward with a clean slate and continue carefully tossing the sticks into the fire. Watch the flames absorb them until the pile is entirely gone.

8. Smile upon the warmth before you and thank the energies that push us forward.

Energy Circles

(To be done in preparation for new adventures)

MATERIALS NEEDED: Flowers, string (optional), ribbon (for poles only), group of friends.

PREPARATION: Best done at Beltane or during the warm season as a group activity. Have the women pick wildflowers and make crowns, necklaces, and or bracelets out of them by tying the stems or attaching them to string. Have the men collect sticks to place around a selected tree or raise the pole so it stays up in the ground and attaches ribbons at the top.

THE WORK:

1. During the festivities, bring everyone together around a designated tree or pole.

2. For a tree circle, everyone should clasp their hands. For the pole, everyone needs to hold an end of the ribbon.

3. Give the group a moment to clear their minds and focus on building energy to welcome new ideas, opportunities, and lives.

4. When ready, slowly begin to circle the tree or pole. Steady at first, slowly pick up the pace. Let your energy build. Speed up and sing, laugh, or chant together.

5. Continue until dizzy, like a child. Then sit together and meditate. Breathe easy and relax your mind.

6. Let whatever thoughts enter your mind draw new ideas. Allow your mind to wander and be mindful of new ideas.

7. When ready to move on, lay on the ground for a moment before moving on to other celebrations.

Tree Friends

MATERIALS NEEDED: Birdseed or squirrel feed.
PREPARATION: Best done during a waxing moon cycle or Ostara.

THE WORK:

1. Go outside and set a basket/bowl of birdseed or squirrel feed before you under a tree.

2. Sit quietly and meditate. Close your eyes and breathe in your surroundings. Feel the energy surrounding you, the atmosphere, and its power.

3. Now open your eyes and carefully scoop some feed into your hands. Gently toss it away from you, or even stand and spread it beneath the tree with a carefree, childish manner.

4. Remain calm and still like the tree sheltering above. If a squirrel or bird comes to feed, keep your distance, and observe their grace. Speak softly and let your energies reach out from your center.

5. When all the food is gone, and the animals have left or distanced themselves bow to the tree and resume other activities.

Seek What Hides

(To be done when feeling lost or in need of direction)

MATERIALS NEEDED: 3-7 Small trinkets. Best to use rocks, sea shells, crystals, or other energy-charged items that mean a lot spiritually.
PREPARATION: Let each item represent unwanted aspects of life or current uncertainty that you are facing. Meditate on the items one by one and visualize overcoming them. Have a friend or loved one count and place these items around your living space or yard, but not too hidden. Do it before Imbolc celebration or on a cloudy day.

THE WORK:

1. Search for the trinkets.
2. Upon finding the first one, kneel before it and take it in your hands. Stare at it. Envision how the issue it represents has affected you.
3. Then glance around. See the entire area in its fullness. Look at the small item and see it for what it really is: a small mass in a greater world.
4. Now seek out the next items. Repeat the previous step with each of them.
5. When all have been found, take them to the foot of a familiar tree and glance up. Imagine the rocks and other geographical formations the tree roots have had to work their way around. Place your hands over the items and feel the warmth inside. Let that energy build.
6. Expand that inner heat throughout your body until it extends from your fingertips and overpowers the trinkets and what they represent.
7. Be mindful of new thoughts. Solutions and routes around your obstacles will present themselves. Take your time to meditate on the different ideas that present themselves. Be patient and willing to redirect your path.

Befriending a Stump

(To be done when experiencing negativity or feeling frustrated)

MATERIALS NEEDED: Nature walk items (flowers, acorns, leaves, twigs, etc.), and a potted plant (optional)

PREPARATION: Take a nature walk and collect items to decorate the base/seat of a stump. Do it on a sunny day as an uplifting ritual to help ward off anxiety and depression.

THE WORK:

1. Bring items before the stump on a sunny day.
2. Place hands on the top and meditate on connecting with the wood.
3. Turn and sit on the stump. Breathe deep and close your eyes. Visualize the trunk that once stood tall where you are sitting. Sit as tall as possible and work to exude that towering energy.
4. Open your eyes and stand up. Place the basket in the center of the stump. Take each item out one by one. Set them around the base of the stump in a ring.
5. Now step back to look at the stump.
6. Whisper, chant, or sing of beautifying change to ward off anxieties and depression. Let the warmth inside grow until you feel your energy expanding. Repeat the words until you feel lightheaded.
7. Then bow to the stump and return as often as necessary. Use it as a place of meditation to sit and find comfort.

See Saw Away

(To conquer fear)

MATERIALS NEEDED: A large stick or branch and a small one.

PREPARATION: Do during the waxing moon or on Mabon

THE WORK:

1. Before feasting for Mabon or during a moon rite, place the large stick before the ritual fire. Dangle the small stick over the top facing the opposite direction, making a cross shape while keeping ample space above the large stick lying on the ground. Let go[JB16] .

2. Watch the stick fall and imagine yourself falling into the fear of whatever you struggle to overcome.

3. Now pick it up. Place a hand at one end and carefully lay it across the large stick before the fire. As you do this, envision new ways to face your fear and see yourself doing so without panic or struggle.

4. Pick the stick up again and visualize yourself overcoming your fear step-by-step.

5. Slowly set it down again and repeat this process. Each time you pick the stick up, focus on reducing stress.

6. Hold the small stick out over the big one on the ground again. Let it go and watch it fall. Smile and draw strength from the simple act of playing with what you can control. Feel how it warms you, boosts your energies

7. Know that you are not a fragile stick. See yourself as the larger stick below it, holding it up.

8. Take the sticks to the ritual fire and toss them in. Bow to the energies shared and enjoy a feast, but don't forget what you've learned.

Stick in the Mud

(To see the future or find answers)

MATERIALS NEEDED: Stick, a puddle of mud
PREPARATION: Do under the full moon's light or during Samhain

THE WORK:

1. Meditate on the stick. Build your energies with the warmth inside and send that heat into the stick.

2. Go before the puddle and stand, sit, or kneel, whatever allows you to stir the water comfortably. Now stir the water in a counter-clockwise motion. Have fun just playing in the water for a while.

3. Looks at the ripples created. Watch them and look for patterns. Images or words may appear. Be aware of how this motion affects you and your thoughts.

4. Be perceptive to new ideas. Let these thoughts take you on a journey as you explore your mind, but remain relaxed and open to what you see, think, and feel.

5. Flashes of the past or future may come to you. Current events in the present might reveal themselves in the cool liquid. However, as these manifest, remain calm and fluid in your stirring.

6. Stay encouraged if nothing apparent comes directly. Sometimes it is the after-effects of these motions that matter most. Continue to stir until you become dizzy or lightheaded. Then, bow to the water, take the stick to the fire, place it beneath a tree, and gaze up at the sky above the branches.

Carving Names

(To remember a loved one)

MATERIALS NEEDED: Pocket knife or plaque to set.

PREPARATION: Take time to heal. Losing a loved one is never easy, but honoring them is an essential aspect of being.

THE WORK:

1. On the next birthday of the person or animal who has passed away, or a special day that meant a lot to you both, either host a plaque dedication or carve their initials and a symbol that represents them into the bark of a familiar tree.

2. Place your hand over the letters and mourn for the loss. Think of all you will miss, and don't be afraid to express your sorrow.

3. Now, kneel before the memorial and recall your happiest memory of that person or creature.

4. Raise hands toward the branches and gaze from the tree roots, up the bark, and through the tree line up to the sky. Let the love and the happy moments radiate power. Smile and laugh and think of all that you shared, feeling the warmth of your bond.

5. Once more, place your hand over the letters and cry or smile, both if possible. Feel the energy that ties us all to our birth and death, and respect it. Think of being children together and the innocence that brings.

6. Bow to the memorial. Thank the tree. Return to it often, and never forget the one you love.

3

TREE SPELLS FOR
THE INNER CHILD

TREES INSPIRE POWER. THEY CRAFT AND SWAY ENERGIES based on the needs of their environment. The voice within adheres to this form of magic. It is more apt to be released without fear or judgment when returning to a simpler mindset.

Defining specific needs and harnessing the elements that strengthen trees is more manageable when approached from a position of growth. Focusing the senses on change and smooth transition drives spellwork toward more tangible success. Instead of becoming enraptured by unrealistic fantasies, this approach leads to more long-term realizations. When I run around with my children and keep my thoughts on the simple beauty of nature, I develop a great bond with the real world. It becomes easier to focus and enjoy life.

Whimsical Roots

MATERIALS NEEDED: A familiar tree, basket of flowers, nuts, outdoor items, a glass of chocolate milk/juice/water

PREPARATION: Take a nature walk and gather items like flowers, nuts, twigs, and anything that speaks to you and draws the eye.

THE WORK:

1. Take the basket of items you collected with your drink and sit at the foot of a friendly tree.

2. Place your hands over the basket and pool your energies. Let the heat within grow and expand throughout your body. Then work to push that warm energy into the items in the basket.

3. When ready, place these small outdoor items in a circle around the tree's base. As you do, focus on connecting with the beauty of simplicity.

4. Now, sit back and raise your drink to the tree. Call upon the powers of the elements and your gods.

5. Take one single sip of your drink. Let the flavor sit in your mouth. Feel the refreshment as it goes down. Think of childhood treats and how they energized you when you were young, how the smallest treat could mean so much.

6. Now pour a small sprinkle of your drink on the ground before the tree. Take your time and drink the rest of the contents.

Recall your childhood dreams and the ideas that transformed you with each sip.

7. Reminisce and remember who you grew up from.

Log Roll Spell

MATERIALS NEEDED: Fairly sized log of at least three feet and pocketknife or dagger (for carving)

PREPARATION: Obtain a large log and meditate on your dagger or pocketknife as a vessel of your will. Create a sigil or symbol to represent the change needed.

THE WORK:

1. Place the log at one end of the yard, field, or open space.

2. Kneel before it and place both of your hands upon the wood.

3. Feel the heat within and let it flow throughout your body. Build those energies and push them into the log.

4. Now, visualize the issue that deters you from accepting change. See it clearly and whisper, chant, or sing of turning it over on its head to resolve it.

5. Take the pocket knife or dagger and carve your symbol or sigil into the log. Take your time, and be careful. The image does not have to resemble the work of a great artist.

6. When finished carving, close the blade and set it aside or place it in your pocket. Now stand before the log and look down at it. See it as the change needing to be made and roll it forward.

7. Stop. Take a breath. Now roll it twice as far. Pause, take another breath, and push it as far as you can, moving your hands again and again. Feel your power shifting the log and taking charge of the weight it has presented you with.

8. Once you have reached the end of the space, stop and stand the log on one end in an upright position. Do not be alarmed if it falls.

9. Step back. Close your eyes and feel the change coming. Breathe deep and embrace it.

Leaf Bed Protection

(To retain peace during chaos)

MATERIALS NEEDED: Pile of leaves

PREPARATION: Rake your yard or push a bunch of leaves into a pile during autumn.

THE WORK:

1. Jog around the pile to clear the mind. Let the crisp air fill your lungs. Build your energies as your body warms against the chill.

2. Now stop before the leaves.

3. Focus on your heartbeat. Place your right hand over it. Close your eyes.

4. Kneel down slowly and reach forward. Hold your right hand over the leaf pile and envision your warm energies flowing into the leaves. See that energy as a light that illuminates them.

5. Now open your eyes and gently turn/fall forward. Roll into the leaves and let them encompass you.

6. Lay on your back and grab handfuls to cover yourself with. Smile, laugh at yourself, and know that you are cared for and connected to the trees and plants surrounding you.

Splitting Sticks to Break Bad Habits

(To dispel negative habits)

MATERIALS NEEDED: Bundle/pile of sticks, a fire pit of hearth, matches or lighter

PREPARATION: Collect sticks. Perform during a waning moon cycle or new moon.

THE WORK:

1. Pick up a stick from the pile. Grasp it tight and think of the habit you wish to break.

2. Visualize the stick as an unnecessary or negative behavior.

3. Feel the heat within you and work to push it through your limbs. Let the energies flow. Build that great warm power within until you feel ready to burst. Then clearly envision yourself ending the habit.

4. Break the stick in two and place it in the fire pit or fire space.

5. Repeat until you have enough sticks to successfully light a fire.

6. Stand before the broken sticks with your matches or lighter and raise your arms to the sky. Whisper, chant, or sing of breaking the cycle to move onward into a better future.

7. Now light the fire.

8. Watch it burn and feel your energies shift. Let your spirit grow wholly connected to this plan. Fully commit.

9. When exhausted, sit before the flames or the ashes if they have died down. Bow your head and breathe deep.

Beneath the Trees
for the Future

(To prepare for the future and protect younger generations)

MATERIALS NEEDED: Seeds or flowers for shade planting (or partial shade, depending on the area), a small garden shovel, and a pocket knife or dagger.

PREPARATION: Create a sigil or symbol that represents preserving the integrity of the future/new generations.

THE WORK:

1. Gather your materials beneath a tree.

2. Place your hands on the ground and connect your energies to the tree's soil and roots that will guard the new sprouts.

3. Now take up your shovel and dig a ring around the tree. Drop in your seeds or plant new bulbs around the base. Then bury and pack the soil.

4. Wait a week.

5. Return to the tree and stand before the ring. Take your pocket knife or dagger to the east side of the tree. Gently carve your symbol or sigil in the soil before the seeds/plants.

6. Do this on the North, West, and South side in that order.

7. When finished, return to the east side and face the tree. Gaze from its base, up the trunk, to the branches. Think of childhood and its wonder. Meditate on how growth begins in youth.

8. Refocus your thoughts on the ring of flowers you planted. Pat the earth and bow to it. Whisper, chant, or sing of the seeds' possibilities.

9. Last, place your palms on the soil and ground yourself in the present. Smile and be content.

Vine Swing Spell

(To overcome fear or sway outcomes)

MATERIALS NEEDED: Sturdy vine or rope swing.

PREPARATION: Take a walk in a familiar wooded area and test out safe vines by just tugging on them and carefully adding more weight OR create/use a backyard rope swing with a knot at the end for balance.

THE WORK:

1. Place both hands on the vine. Bow your head and close your eyes.

2. Whisper, chant, or sing for guidance. As the words come, let the heat within expand. Build the power within yourself.

3. Now grasp the vine and draw back just a step or two. Speak of swaying yourself or the outcomes you're uncertain of. Lift your feet and swing.

4. Regain your footing and repeat, but this time step farther back, drawing more tension on the vine/rope. Lift your feet and swing as carefree as a kid.

5. Perform a 3rd time, but go back as far as the vine/rope will allow and focus on attacking your fear/the unknown head-on. Let the air cradle you. Let the unknown guide you.

6. Regain footing and let go of the vine/rope. Bow to it and smile or laugh. Now sit nearby and place your palms on the ground to rebalance yourself and focus on the present.

Climbing Collection
for Health

(To be done during harvest season. Some trees bear fruit in early summer, while others do so in fall. Plan accordingly)

MATERIALS NEEDED: Fruit or nut trees, basket or bucket, ladder (optional), hose or water tank (optional)

PREPARATION: This is for individuals who have planted their own fruit and nut trees or have friends or family with fruit or nut trees. Pluck easy-to-reach fruit or nuts with friends or family members who are unable to climb if possible

THE WORK:

1. Stand before the bare lower branches of the tree. Gaze up at the foods that are out of reach. Relax your body and clear your mind.

2. Find a sturdy branch and climb up, or set up a ladder and go up 1 step. Seek out a hearty branch full of offerings, pick the fruit, and drop it down.

3. Sing, chant, or whisper thanks for the tree's gifts as you gather the fruit into a basket or bucket.

4. Repeat this all the way from the north, south, east, and west until the tree empties its heavy load.

5. Carry your pickings inside to be washed if at home or to a hose or water tank if elsewhere. As you cleanse the foods, visualize the nutrients they hold and how they will benefit you and everyone who consumes them.

6. Take them home and think of how these foods nourish your body.

Think of how they helped you grow as a child. Then use these foods in your next meal.

Sharing for Confidence

(To dispel self-consciousness)

MATERIALS NEEDED: A favorite book, journal, or memorized passages of meaningful writing

PREPARATION: Become as familiar with the words as possible

THE WORK:

1. Go before a familiar tree and place your left hand on the trunk. Hold your book, journal, or palm up on your right hand and slowly circle the tree, keeping your left hand touching it the entire time, dragging your palm over the surface.

2. Begin reading or reciting from the book/journal and keep walking. Let the tree balance and guide you as you express your energies of emotional connection.

3. Find a line of phrase that profoundly resonates with you. Repeat these favored words three times and keep walking, drawing more energy out and around you. Let your head grow light but keep your feet steady.

4. Then stop and face the tree. Close your eyes and breathe deeply.

5. Turn away from the tree and look out. Again, breathe deep and feel the love and light of self-expression and being in nature. Visualize this positive moment repeating and calming the air. Now sit and ground and smile at the tree before moving on.

Bark Decoration
Beautification Spell

(To find and share inner beauty)

MATERIALS NEEDED: Strings of leaves, large unclosed wrath of branches, ribbon, and flower strings. (Enough for self and tree)

PREPARATION: String leaves and/or flowers, tie wreath branches together but leave them open for clasping around the tree trunk. Best done on Midsummer.

THE WORK:

1. Bring your materials before the tree you wish to decorate.
2. Meditate on the strings, wreath(s), and ribbons. Run fingers over the materials to better connect them to your purpose. Let their beauty and simplicity calm your spirit and balance your being.
3. Now arrange and tie the strings and wreaths around the trunk and lay them through branches to suit your tastes. Work in the ribbons.
4. Next, arrange strings, wreaths, and ribbons upon yourself and any other participants if working in a group.
5. Dance, sing, and circle the tree. Gaze at its beauty and think of how its beauty is connected to you. Feel the warmth inside and let it grow. Push that energy out toward the tree.
6. Now visualize yourself as you are, and look to the tree to realize your own beauty. Focus on how the tree's decorations do not entirely change it and that nature needs no decorations to be beautiful, just as you do not.
7. Remember when you felt beautiful as a child and how that affected your experiences.

8. Slowly remove the decorations from yourself. Then and untie them from the tree. Watch the branches bounce back and rejoice at regaining their true form.

9. Rub your hands over your arms and legs and feel your skin as it should be. Let it breathe, and smile. Burn the decorations in a fire during a ceremony or at your next ritual.

TREE PLANTING
ENERGY

THERE ARE MANY TYPES OF GROWTH. HUMAN GROWTH often branches beyond physicality and the tangible world. To become whole, we must connect to more than what we can hold and see, but the power of touch is a magnificent link that connects us to many different planes of existence. As a child, I could sense animals living in the trees long before they made themselves known. This allowed me to walk with gentle steps so as not to frighten them.

That aided so many of my youthful experiences. I spent a great deal of time exploring the woods and creeks around my apartment complex as well as climbing trees. Because of this, I fine-tuned my senses to pick up on subtleties that many other people rarely recognized.

My connection to plants and animals deepened as my brain developed. I became more aware and knew how to predict behaviors likely to occur during hikes and outings.

That great understanding tapped into something much more powerful than myself. Instead of remaining scientific (which is merely one crucial element of understanding), intuition and personal energy fused my spiritual perception with the physical. When people freely open themselves up to the wild languages, a new calling is heard. Our energies can flow outside of ourselves. That personal power strengthens our ability to empathize and understand greater possibilities that reach beyond a singular consciousness or existence.

Planting is one of the best ways to strengthen this bond. Seeking knowledge from flowers and a small brush is helpful, but looking to the trees allows us to fully recognize the larger scale of history and our place in the world. Our senses awaken to spirits, ancestral ties, and self-awareness. Exploring these avenues creates an internal compass that better directs our thoughts and actions.

We find a new appreciation for life. Our origin and that of the creatures around us become more important, and saplings and seeds burst with magic. These tiny beings hold the potential to grow beyond our expectations, yet they can only sprout with the combined effort of proper elements.

Planting a tree cultivates our spiritual nature. It gifts one hope, pride, and a sense of purpose. To find the right spot, kneel down, and dig a hole, knowing that your efforts could long outlast yourself in the form of a great wooden giant puts the material world in perspective. Yes, trees, in the physical sense, are a great necessity, but something within them also speaks to our spiritual selves.

They tap into an ancient source that humans are less likely to come across. When roots connect with elder trees, the vibrations can be picked up on. Communications and the atmosphere seem clearer. Our ability to know and trust grows more profound with the newly formed roots.

There is a familiarity that also comes with the magic of trees. For years now, I have visited familiar forests seeking old friends. I see faces in the trees and feel their power and energy.

Some people believe that humans look for faces in nature, and that's what makes them appear. Pattern recognition is a crucial aspect of human thought, and it is true. Though not everyone can pinpoint the exact science behind this, finding faces in plants and objects was once labeled pareidolia. It was deemed a mental state where individuals saw things that did not exist, but modern research discovers that there is more to this phenomenon than imagination or cognitive differences.

Jessica Taubert of the U.S. National Institute of Mental Health and Catherine Mondloch of Brock University in Ontario are utilizing Ronald Senack's fieldwork to connect how seeing faces in inanimate objects, plants, and other scenes may be a sign of intense emotion. While Kang Lee at the University of Toronto has studied links between this behavior and creativity or even heightened perception. In every modern study on this subject, where faces are seen in trees, the tree itself is either aged or has been injured. There is no explanation for this. It is as if these lifelike images are drawn forth over time or from a destructive experience.

I believe that, like humans, trees gain more personality throughout the years or after experiencing trauma. In my findings, those who seek to find deeper connections in life are more likely to recognize faces where others do not believe they exist.

Everywhere I have lived, I found myself drawn to the plant life in my area, specifically the trees and the shapes they present. When gazing out the front window of my first house, the face of the Green god stared back at me through the massive pin oak in my front yard. It did not matter what season it was, whether the leaves were green, gold, or bare. In winter, the sleepy eyes shook in the wind. During spring, the God tossed the sleep from his eyes and squinted at me. In summer, his bushy beard regrew to turn orange at the fall harvest.

The gods have followed me wherever I go. It doesn't matter where one resides; if their heart is open, they will find life smiling back at them. Midsummer spirits call from bushes and firelight, Mabon mysteries make themselves known, but it is the voice and following of our ancestors that is most impactful.

One's heritage aids them on their spiritual journey. No matter where a person is from or who they share familial ties with, there are lessons to be found and utilized in examining where they came from and looking to the future with confidence in who they are.

My grandfather's grandmother was Indigenous to America. There is little information known about her. No one passed down stories about who she was other than what she was because it was taboo for my grandfather to ask about her when he was a child. This family mystery has built a bond from curiosity, and that alone runs wild within me.

To be at peace with who we are does not always mean knowing everything or even anything about our family tree. Sometimes, people know something as sure as their own name without being taught it. This intuition lives within all of us. This often manifests through the healing practices I prefer to use over modern medicines. How to tend to certain illnesses or what herbs to incorporate for good health have allowed me to test my knowledge of unsourced information.

At times, it bridges the gap between generations and leads beyond the physical realm as we know it. Because I had a great love for my maternal grandparents, who taught me so much, I can better communicate with them even though they are not of this earth anymore. I have no medium powers. My ability to conjure dead relatives is non-existent, yet still, they are present in my life because they come to me in the trees and the wisdom that naturally enters my thoughts.

Outside of my home sit three massive trees. One is perfect for climbing and spaced away from the other two, but the pair that twist and reach into the sky around each other have come to represent Tom and Betty Lawless: my grandparents, the elders in my life who gave me the gift of love and a thirst for knowledge and understanding.

One is tall and towering, like my grandfather. It looms at times, but always with a protective eye. On calm mornings in July (near his birthday), I can hear his voice, his spirit communicating through the shellbark hickory. It guides me through uncertainty and praises my courageous spirit.

The other hickory's trunk is shorter and fatter. Branches jet out much further down than their partner, giving it a more rounded maternal appearance. I cannot see anything but my grandmother when I stare at it. She was a pudgy little Irish American lady who mothered eight children. She does not consciously visit as often as grandpa does, I believe she has too many places to check on, but when she does, I feel the same sense of calm that occurred while sitting with her and talking or doing puzzles together.

These experiences have taught me that no matter how a person sees the trees, there are lines of communication waiting to be found. Tree planting and communication meditations host gateways and new revelations. Rituals and spellwork further awaken new energies and help us speak through the trees.

4

TREE PLANTING/ COMMUNICATION MEDITATIONS

Planting trees and using them to communicate with the natural world is holy work. It leaves behind denominations and division. The practitioner must selflessly accept what is revealed with complete trust in the universe. Digging below the earth's surface to root something new is a perfect time to hone in on personal energies and extend powers. Not all of my planting projects are successful, which is part of this process. I have seen entire plants spring up only to degrade in the next season. I have planted trees that barely had a chance to live, but the loss of a sapling can draw revelations from the surrounding trees. Some tree communications host more desirable outcomes without ever having to break ground. These are more difficult to achieve because there is less of a physical connection to draw instincts forth and awaken the subconscious spirit, but practice and will drive successful meditations.

Seed Starting Meditation

(For growth/exploration. Best done in spring or summertime)

Step 1: Take the seed to the area it will be planted.

Step 2: Place it in the palm of your hand and focus on the potential that lives in the tiny being. Let the warmth inside it expand and reach you. Focus on pulling the plants' energies outward for better growth.

Step 3: Gently rub the seed with the forefinger of your opposite hand. While you do this, meditate on the air, the atmosphere, and any new thoughts which spring to mind. Think about the questions that surface. Then direct your thoughts on why a single seed holds importance and what its purpose means to you.

Step 4: Now cup your opposite hand over the palm holding the seed and close your eyes. Visualize the seed sprouting, thriving, and rooting in the soil that will surround it. Focus on the comfort of the earth, tightening its hold to offer guidance and support through the darkness.

Step 5: Direct your attention to yourself. Think of the endeavors you are embarking on or considering. Let the warmth inside you build and grow. Let it inspire images that connect you and the seed, all life.

Step 6: Now, open your eyes, kneel or sit on the ground and dig a hole for the seed. Feel the soil with your hands. Allow your skin to push and pull the earth as needed.

Step 7: Place the seed in the hole and gaze upon it with hopes for a balanced life. Accept that it may thrive or it may not. Conditions and circumstances sometimes stunt growth, but there are times when nothing will mar existence. Will yourself to smile at the possibilities.

Step 8: Fill in the hole and pat the ground, contemplating this future. Meditate on it from a personal level. See yourself growing like the seed and follow that trail beyond yourself into a broader, more connected universe.

Step 9: Pull yourself back to reality when feeling dizzy or light-headed. Lay down in the dirt nearby or grass and breathe deep to ground your conscious self.

Easy Tree Planting Meditation

(To be done in the spring for stronger bonds with nature)

Step 1: Find the sapling that speaks to you and bring it to its proper planting home.

Step 2: Kneel before the sapling and study its small branches, immature trunk, and buds that have just begun to live.

Step 3: Place your hands on the ground where it will be planted. Envision the nutrients and creatures below who will help or hinder the sapling's rise into the sky.

Step 4: Now dig the hole to plant the tree in. Ensure it is deep enough and in an area with proper drainage/moisture and sunlight/shade.

Step 5: Take the young tree out of its temporary housing and examine the roots. Cup a hand under them and study the intricate web of life that already thrives. Think of how complex even the simplest lives can become and how the trees rely on us and we rely on them.

Step 6: Place the roots into the hole and fill it with dirt. As you do so, visualize the elements that nourish your life. Who and what do you need to be who you need to be?

Step 7: Pat the earth around the newly planted sapling. Feel its energies shifting. Absorb what power you need and expel what you can to aid the tree itself.

Step 8: Close your eyes and place your fingertips on the trunk. Be attentive to the atmosphere; the changes inside of yourself. What thoughts spring from the crust of your being? What toxins are revealed that need to be expelled? Follow this journey.

Step 9: When exhausted, sit back and smile at the tree. Wish it well and rub its branches. Then move on.

Focused Tree Planting Meditation

(To be done in honor of a loved one who has passed on)

Step 1: When planting in honor of a loved one who has passed on, bring the seed(s) or sapling into your home where you are most comfortable and either hold or touch it (them). Build the energies within. Focus on utilizing your strength and your love for the person now missing from your physical life to transform this young plant into a great healthy being.

Step 2: Take the tree or seed(s) where it (they) will be planted. Stand where you will plant it and gaze up to the sky. Close your eyes while keeping hold of the sapling or seed(s). Feel the warmth inside you and let it stretch throughout your body. Push that energy out to the plant and down through the ground. Envision the roots taking hold, the trunk growing tall and wide, and the tree blossoming into a pillar of memory and unbreakable bonds.

Step 3: Now step back, kneel down, and dig the hole. Place the seed(s) or sapling in its rightful spot. Then fill in the rest of the hole and gently pack the dirt on top.

Step 4: Sit before the tree and think of the person you miss: what they meant to you, how they changed the course of your life. Imagine their energies being shared with the trees as all beings flow through life and death in a connected environment.

Step 5: Remain for as long as you need to feel at peace. Then, breathe deep and walk on.

Planting for Peace

(Best done in spring to find balance and appreciate life)

Step 1: Obtain the seed or sapling desired for an area best suited for it. Before planting, sit on the spot where the tree will grow. Look around. Glance up at the sky. Become conscious of the elements, the moisture, the air, the sun (or lack thereof), and the spark of life surrounding the space.

Step 2: Lay down on your back. Close your eyes and breathe deeply. Embrace the peace that comes with lying on the earth. Let that calming energy wrap around you, and focus on your senses. Feel the warmth inside and let it fill your body.

Step 3: Listen to everything around you and even your own pulse. Does the ground host any powerful shifts or unspoken messages that surface? Does the seedling or seed call out to you or laugh like a child? Explore the thoughts and images that come to mind in this state.

Step 4: Open your eyes and roll onto your side. Talk to the tree as if you were talking to yourself. Allow your instincts to direct your actions. Get up when ready and move the seed or sapling as needed. Dig a hole with a sense of self and calming love.

Step 5: Place the tree into the hole and feel the dirt surrounding it. Breathe in the musty tones. Smile at the calm nature. Then, fill in the space and pat the soil.

Step 6: Lie down on your stomach and face the tree. Keep breathing deep, and close your eyes. Visualize the peaceful new plant properly rooted before you. Revel in that wonder and enjoy your hand in bringing it to its rightful home.

Planting to Connect Beyond

(For spring planting, to strengthen spiritual ties)

Step 1: Select the sapling that best suits your personality. Let it represent you as more than just a person

Step 2: Bring it to the space where it will be planted and sit quietly.

Step 3: Focus on each of your senses individually. Breathe deep and close your eyes. Open your mouth to taste the air. Experience the particles floating unseen as you never have before.

Step 4: Close your mouth and flare your nostrils. Become conscious of your olfactory prowess. Hone in on it. What scents cling to the world around you, and what stories do they tell?

Step 5: Relax your face and tilt your head. Really listen to the world and all its muffled cries. Allow your inner voice to speak if it presents itself.

Step 6: Sit tall and open your eyes. Instead of just looking, really scan everything before you. Notice the shadows, the vegetation's reaction to the weather, and any animal movements that catch the eye. Too often, we see without recognizing detail. Let these indications make themselves known and guide you.

Step 7: Once more, close your eyes, and place your hands on the ground in front of you. Walk your fingertips back and forth. Make yourself feel more. How does the air caress your face? How does the surface beneath you affect your body and your energies? What pangs or sensations rise from your core? Feel them and let them offer insight.

Step 8: Repeat these steps with the tree you wish to plant. Going through each sense but incorporating the tree-to-be. Each sense opens a gateway when properly utilized. This meditation is just a link between yourself and the being you are planting.

Step 9: When finished with these meditations, dig a hole and plant the tree, enjoying sensory perception. Then pat the earth once finished and return to meditate as the tree grows.

Listening to the Trees

(*For inspiring new ideas*)

Step 1: Take a walk in a heavily wooded forest area.

Step 2: Focus on each sense individually. First, open your mouth and taste the air. Close your mouth, breathe deeply, and focus on the scents wafting in. Are there pine, hickory, or palm? What do these natural perfumes say?

Step 3: Keep your experience in mind, but shift the focus to what you hear. Not just the animals but the sounds produced by swaying branches or shifting leaves.

Step 4: Stop walking and step aside if you're on a path. Close your eyes. Be like the trees. How do they communicate and thrive? It all starts from the ground up. Muse on that for a few moments.

Step 5: Open your eyes again. Bend down and touch the dirt that lies before you. Feel more than just its dusty aspect. Reach further.

Step 6: Walk off the path into the trees. Touch their trunks, limbs, sticks, and growths. You will experience more than you did before. The trees may send you sensations, vibrations, or even new ideas.

Step 7: Continue your walk and ponder what you learned

Talking to the Trees

(*To be done each morning to build a greater sense of consciousness and appreciation for life*)

Step 1: Dedicate time every morning to walk among the trees surrounding your home and commit to doing this for at least 10 days uninterrupted.

Step 2: Go to the first tree, stand right in front of the trunk and place palms on the bark with fingers facing up. Close your eyes and breathe deeply. Exhale and gaze up the trunk to the treetop.

Step 3: Say good morning to the tree and offer up hopes or well wishes for the day. Pat the trunk and move on to another nearby tree (if you have more than 1).

Step 4: Do this until all the trees have been spoken to. After a few days, revelations, vibrations, and sensations will root within. You will experience the response in different ways.

Step 5: Continue with more flexibility once that period is complete.

Searching the Trees

(To strengthen powers of observation)

Step 1: Go hiking or walk through a heavily wooded area. Breathe deep and easy.

Step 2: Look down and focus on stepping in rhythm. Glance around the forest floor. Scan the tree roots that stick up and tree trunks growing before you as you walk.

Step 3: Now look up at the tree canopy ahead. Keep your vision focused forward to retain the walking rhythm, but relax your mind and study the light filtering through the trees. Look at how the branches and leaves connect as if its own internet. Keep walking and watching, shifting your eyes slightly to ensure you can see as you go along, and be attentive to the tree life overhead.

Step 4: Patterns, shapes, or images may reveal themselves above. Sensations or vibrations often reach out easier. If goosebumps appear on your skin, your ears start ringing, or you feel called to a particular area, stop and commune with it internally.

Step 5: Continue walking when ready and repeat as you go.

Walking Beyond the Trees

(To become more aware of the spirit realm and alternate realities beyond what we know)

Step 1: Find a comfortable space anywhere. Inside or out. Find your happiest place to be and go there.

Step 2: Walk in a circle. Small or large, just make sure the area is cleared, and you know it well so you can focus your mind instead of watching out for things to bump into.

Step 3: Let the energy build. Relax your mind and visualize your favorite tree. Smell it and taste its scent in the air. Hear the wind in the boughs until you see it so clearly in your mind that you can touch it.

Step 4: Reach for it only in spirit as you continue walking. Feel the bark. Let it transform you and lead your consciousness beyond your current physical realm.

Step 5: Streaks of color or light may appear before you. Let the trance continue as your energies lock into the circle you continue to walk.

Step 6: Open your senses and listen to what is sent to you. Allow the visions that need to break through. Stop before your body becomes too fatigued. This is generally when walking the path becomes difficult.

Step 7: Sit down and center your mind on reality. Relax and contemplate what you experienced.

5

———

TREE RITUALS FOR COMMUNICATION

G ROWTH IS A CONSTANT RITUAL. WHETHER ONE ACKNOWLEDGES it or not, it is unstoppable. We can either grow upward or doddle in between. I have always looked to the trees when feeling down. Timber's tenacity and persistence stood before me when I was most alone. It led to a perfect example when walking away from abuse, coping with loss, and venturing into unfamiliar territory.

Communicating with trees is a ritual unto itself. How one reaches out, absorbs, and performs the act of taking the time to open the sense and fully experience nature finds that their energies are more personalized and positive. Planting offers new hopes and new beginnings. It bonds one to their existence. Everyone is welcome to customize or alter the rituals listed as they need. There are many methods for planting and communicating with trees regularly, but performing acts that better connect us to the trees and the natural world hosts many benefits.

Seed Blessing

(To ensure growth)

MATERIALS NEEDED: Half-filled cup of water, seed, and a small container of dirt.

PREPARATION: Do within a short period between obtaining the seed(s) and planting. Best done between Beltane and Lammas.

THE WORK:

1. Place the water to the left and the dirt to the right in front of you. Place the seed in the middle.

2. Take up the seed and hold it over the water cup. Acknowledge the power of water (through thought, words, song, etc.). Truly meditate on it. Then drop the seed in. Watch it float down.

3. Take up the dirt and hold it over the water. Acknowledge the power of earth (through thought, words, song, etc.). Focus on what a bit of earth can do. Now dump the dirt into the water covering the seed.

4. Grasp the cup containing all these elements and hold it up, blessing them with the power of air and sun. Place it in the center of the altar until ready for planting (best done within the day).

Ancestral Tree Planting

(To honor your heritage)

MATERIALS NEEDED: Sapling, instrument(s) or object(s) that has been passed down through generations (can be a utensil, jewelry, photo, song, saying, or more), planting space, and digging tools.

PREPARATION: Meditate just before starting, focusing on your parents, grandparents, and as far back as you remember. Best done on or around Midsummer.

THE WORK:

1. Place the sapling to your left and kneel before the spot where it will be planted.

2. Hold the ancestral object(s) close. Now think of phrases or songs popularly used within your family for generations. Sing or say those words.

3. Now, turn to the sapling and adorn it with your familial objects.

4. Turn back to the space and dig the hole, focusing your energies on who you are and where you came from.

5. Take up the tree and plant it in this space.

6. If you can/are willing to do so, bury the item(s) or just one of the objects with the roots. Think of the generations that came before you as you do this and how the seeds we sow today benefit younger generations.

7. Pat the earth and close your eyes. Call upon your ancestors to find you through this sacred tree. Ask the gods to grant it the power to become a communication vessel.

8. Be still and clear your mind. Wait for new thoughts to enter and

answers to come to you.

9. Now, stand up and breathe deeply while raising your arms to the sky.

10. Slowly bring your arms back down and gaze upon the sapling with new eyes. Return to the tree every day for at least an entire season.

Sealed Roots

(To seek solutions to complex issues)

MATERIALS NEEDED: Paper, pen, gardening shovel, and a tree
PREPARATION: Best done on Mabon or Samhain.

THE WORK:

1. Go to a familiar/trusted tree with materials. Sit at the roots and focus on their ability to maintain a plant that towers above the dirt.

2. Let recent concerns, woes, and issues surface in your mind. Contemplate them. Sift through the rational and irrational.

3. Now, write down the questions or concerns that cannot be easily resolved.

4. Fold up the paper and dig a hole before the tree. Place a hand at its base and thank the tree for sheltering you.

5. Ask for aid with your issue(s), place the paper in the hole and bury it.

6. Pack the earth down and visualize burying the topic(s)/issue once and for all.

7. Bow to the tree.

Morning Tree Ritual

(For a more profound connection with nature)

MATERIALS NEEDED: Cup of milk, a small spoon of honey, cinnamon

PREPARATION: Get up with the sun and greet the day with love. Best done on Midsummer or Lammas.

THE WORK:

1. Before eating breakfast, go to the nearest tree to your home. Place the items at the base and step back with the milk.

2. Bid the tree and its kind good morning, then circle it slowly, pouring the milk as close to the roots as possible.

3. Then take up the spoon and offer the tree a compliment, then circle it slowly, drizzling the honey as close to the roots as possible.

4. Next, take the cinnamon and shake it as you slowly circle the tree as close to the roots as possible, asking it to enjoy the day and offer its love.

5. Bow to the wooden giant and breathe deep. Feel your energies swell, and peace expand.

Afternoon Tree Conjure

(To appreciate life and find purpose)

MATERIALS NEEDED: Jar of water, a small cup of salt, and a basket of flower petals

PREPARATION: Best done on Ostara or Beltane.

THE WORK:

1. After lunchtime, go to your favorite tree and place the materials at its feet. Step back and marvel at the giant before you.

2. Dip your fingertips in the water and press them to the trunk. Slowly slide them down the wood grains all the way to the ground and bid the tree good afternoon.

3. Dip your fingertips in the water again, stand up and press your fingertips to your face. Slowly slide them down your features and body all the way to your feet, focusing on sharing the power that emanates from the tree.

4. Now take up the cup of salt and sprinkle it around the tree, reminding it of the salts and minerals that connect everything.

5. Stand still once more and sprinkle salt upon your feet. Wiggle your toes with the grains allowing the purity and sanctity to draw more from the soil into you.

6. Last, take up the flower basket and gently drop handfuls of petals around the tree trunk. Love the petals for their fleeting purpose before they wither.

7. Now sit before these decorative symbols of life renewed and take up the remaining petals. Gently drop them over your head and let them shower your hair and body. Feel the beauty of life caress you and conjure a new spark for what is to come. Rest with the tree and play with the petals for as long as needed.

Starry Tree Scry

(To reveal the future)

MATERIALS NEEDED: Tree, clear sky, fire (optional)
PREPARATION: Best done on Yule or Imbolc.

THE WORK:

1. Step out and breathe in deeply. If possible, build a small fire near a familiar/trusted tree in a fire pit or controlled area.

2. Gaze up through the boughs. Relax your eyes and watch the shadows of the leaves mingle with the stars and/or moonlight poking through the treetop.

3. Keep your eyes fixed on this scene but slowly kneel down and sit comfortably. Breathe deep and clear your mind while keeping your vision eased.

4. Let the calm overtake you. Lay back with your focus still directed up, and place your hands behind your head.

5. Watch the dark figure above shift and move under the sky. Keep breathing deep and let your mind explore the patterns or shapes that reveal themselves to you through the darkened leaves and night beams.

6. If questions or thoughts come to mind, explore them, and let them lead. The answers are waiting in the nighttime solace. The truths you seek are waiting above with the tree.

7. Let this journey run its course until you lose your connection/focus or become exhausted. Sit up and gaze around you to regain your bearings. If keeping a fire, let the flames awaken your consciousness.

Knowledge from the Roots

(To bond yourself to a tree and its wisdom)

MATERIALS NEEDED: Needed: Pin and/or sharp dagger/knife to prick finger and cut wood, trusted tree, digging tools.

PREPARATION: Meditate and be sure you are ready for this phase of life.

THE WORK:

1. Kneel before the tree and dig at the roots.
2. Sit back for a moment and breathe deeply. Pool your energies feeling the warmth inside and expanding that heat.
3. Carefully cut a small slit or hole in the root and hold your hand over it. Let the tree know you wish it well and only mean to further bond yourself.
4. Then prick your finger and push a few drops of blood into the slit/hole in the tree root. Hold your hand over it. Let the universe know you will look out for the tree as it offers insight.
5. Re-bury the root and pat the soil. Now turn your back to the trunk and look out at the world with fresh eyes. Visit daily for at least an entire season and keep frequent visits afterward.

Answers in Growth

(To be done when needing aid healing or moving beyond a personal issue)

MATERIALS NEEDED: Dagger or pocketknife, water, honey, garden shovel, injured or old tree in need of some trimming
PREPARATION: Search for a tree with peeling bark, a limb failing, or damaged in a storm or other event. Meditate on your dagger or pocket knife.

THE WORK:

1. Go before the tree and bow to it. Offer your sympathies, explain what issue you are dealing with or damage you have suffered, and lend your support.
2. Cut away any dead bark or branch sections that are suffering. Place the pieces aside and save them.
3. Dribble water over the newly cut wood and seal it with honey. Let the tree know you wish to heal it. In return, ask for guidance with your issue or healing aid for personal damage.
4. Kneel before the tree and bury the dead pieces by the roots to help protect and preserve it. Then turn and sit with your back to the trunk and visualize it healing.
5. Breathe deep, get up, and bow to the tree.

Reaching for Loved Ones

((To communicate with a deceased family member))

MATERIALS NEEDED: Item or photos from the person to reach, their favorite food, or flower bouquet.
PREPARATION: Meditate on the item or photo of the person you seek. Best done at Samhain or during the full moon.

THE WORK:

1. Go before a familiar tree, preferably one that somewhat resembles the loved one in some strange way.

2. Kneel before the tree and hold up the item or photo. Let your energies build. Expand the warmth inside you throughout your body, then push it out to the tree and surrounding area.

3. Ask the tree to offer its power of communication.

4. Now hold up the food or flowers. Chant, sing, or speak of the power of life and nourishing bonds.

5. Decorate the tree with broken-off bits of food or plucked flowers.

6. Bow before the tree and call for the gods to bring your specific loved one closer through the power of the great tree. Be patient. Wait and rest, but the answer may not come immediately. It may be after a few days. Be attentive and watch for signs, symbols, or changes. The more you do this, the more connected you will become and the easier it will be to receive more defined responses.

6

TREE PLANTING/
COMMUNICATING
SPELLS

S PONTANEOUS ENERGIES SHOULD NEVER BE TAKEN FOR GRANTED. Sometimes a tree or plant speaks so loudly that all other thoughts are buried within the roots of what is calling to me. Other times I need to build up confidence in the spells I plan to perform and religiously follow my rituals and meditations to prepare.

Casting energies to impact all planes of existence is different with each work. The need changes just as time and space do. That is why I have included some spells that compliment spontaneous shifts, as well as a few that are simply seasonal refreshers for tree communications.

Planting for Protection

(To get back in touch with childhood energies)

MATERIALS NEEDED: A familiar tree, basket of flowers, nuts, outdoor items, a glass of chocolate milk/juice/water

PREPARATION: Take a nature walk and gather items like flowers, nuts, twigs, and anything that speaks to you and draws the eye.

THE WORK:

1. Take the tree where it will be planted and place it on that very spot. Set the tools and knife before the sapling.
2. Then stand and raise your arms up to the sky. Breathe deep, exhale and look down.
3. Take the salt and sprinkle it, walking around the tree chanting or singing to create a protective circle to enhance the tree's protective powers.
4. Take up the water and flick fingerfuls while walking around the tree, chanting or singing to nourish the tree's protective energies.
5. Take up the cleansing herb and light it. Hold it over the sapling. Then walk around the tree in the opposite direction you did before, singing or chanting of the cleansing powers of balance and protection. Something to the effect of: Let the balance of nature protect this space, lend light and wisdom, and always keep me safe.
6. Smoke cleanse again and once more stand before the sapling, looking upon it. Kneel down and place your hands against the newly formed branches. Close your eyes and focus your energies on connecting your personal power with that of the tree.

7. Slowly sit down and meditate on the person needing protection. Whether you or someone else, make sure the picture is clear and your visualization is as real as the air you breathe.

8. Chant, whisper, or sing words binding the protective energies of the tree to the person in need and take up the pocketknife. Something to the effect of: Oh great strong tree, lend your strength and energy to 'name" who is most in need.

9. Now carve your picture or sigil on the ground while repeating these words as you carve the image at the 4 points of direction around the tree within the circle.

10. Now gently move the sapling off the dig site and turn the earth with the planting tools, creating a large enough hole to accommodate all the roots.

11. Plant the sapling and pat the earth around it.

12. Stand again and raise your arms up, breathing deeply. Then exhale and look at the new tree. Bow to it, thank it and the gods for aiding you, and open the circle.

13. Then sit and press your hands to the ground. Focus on your surroundings and be present in the now.

Planting for Prosperity

(To be done in times of financial struggle)

MATERIALS NEEDED: Salt, water, preferred smoke cleaning herb, a handful of pennies, sapling, digging tools, and pocketknife or dagger

PREPARATION: Gather materials and bring them to the space

where the tree will be planted.

THE WORK:

1. Place the sapling where it will be buried and cast a circle using the salt, water, and cleansing herb.

2. Now sit before the tree and hold the pennies in one palm, cupping the other hand over them and meditate on their meaning. Draw forth your energies and build off the symbology of the shiny coins—how they represent monetary prosperity and how raw materials can be turned into something much greater than their original purpose.

3. Now focus on your need to prosper. Let the warmth inside you build and push it into each coin until they heat up.

4. Now place the coins around the sapling in a ring. They can be as spread out as necessary.

5. Stand before them and raise your arms up, breathing deeply. Sing or chant of the powers of the universe being conducted by the elements through these coins to enhance the tree's ability to prosper and aid those who seek its wisdom and good fortune.

6. Lower your arms and gaze at the soil that will cultivate this need. Bend down, place your palms on the ground just in front of the tree between the nearest coins, and focus on the person/people most in need. Meditate on mingling their energies with that of the tree.

7. Now move the tree slightly and dig a hole for planting. Bury the coins with it, focusing on who needs its aid most.

8. Pat the earth when finished. Gently rub the branches. Bow to the tree and thank it for its wisdom. Look up to the skies and smile at the universe.

9. Ground yourself and return to the tree often to meditate for prosperity.

Fruitful Planting

(For encouraging plant growth)

MATERIALS NEEDED: Fruit tree(s), bush(es), and/or vine(s), pocketknife or dagger, symbol or sigil

PREPARATION: Design a small symbol/sigil representing a healthy, fruitful plant. To be done in spring.

THE WORK:

1. Plant the tree(s), bush(es), or vine(s) in the proper area with care.

2. Every morning for at least 10 days, go before the plant(s) one-by-one and carve your sigil/symbol into the ground, first facing west on the east point on the first day, then facing south from the northern point on the second, and so on, carving the image into the ground just before the plant at one specific point each day.

3. When doing so, sing or speak the simple words that inspired the symbol/sigil as you carve it.

4. Brush fingers from the roots up and meditate on the plant's growth. Visualize it growing healthy and producing fruit.

5. Listen to it. Visions or thoughts of watering or fertilizing with natural elements may present themselves, and you should act accordingly.

6. When ready to move on, stand and seal the spell by saying, "Blessed Be."

Growing Beauty

(To see your beauty and appreciate yourself)

MATERIALS NEEDED: Small pocket mirror, seed(s) or sapling (preferable flowering) to plant, gardening tools, water, salt, preferred herb for cleansing

PREPARATION: Gather materials and bring them to the area where the tree(s) or bushes will be planted.

THE WORK:

1. Place materials in the center of the space where the tree(s) will be planted.

2. Cast a circle with the salt, water, and cleansing herb, then bow before the seed(s) or sapling. Sit before it and examine its/their details.

3. Meditate on the beauty of growth, nature, and the act of planting. Build your energies focusing on the potential for positive change and additional color and nurturing stemming from the immature form.

4. Hold the seed(s) or touch the branches with your palm up and hold your opposite hand facing down. Feel the flow of your energy, blood, and thoughts surging through you.

5. Meditate on the color and beautiful nature of your spirit and all the positive elements that come together to form who you truly are inside and out.

6. Take the mirror and gaze upon yourself. Not just your facial features; move the mirror around your body to view elbows and knees from new angles. Every line, curve, and shape hosts more purpose than you know. Recognize this.

7. Push your energies into the mirror and draw them back out with the full image of truth to help reduce bias and self-consciousness.

8. Hold the mirror behind the seed(s) or sapling at an angle that allows you to look at yourself from behind these tiny beads of hope. See yourself renewed from behind the seed(s)/sapling.

9. Push the warmth inside of you out through your body. Visualize it connecting to others.

10. Then dig the appropriate hole(s) and plant the seed(s) or tree, but bury the mirror as well. Pat the earth and thank the gods for the insights that have and will continue to blossom within.

11. Bow to the tree, open the circle and ground yourself. Return as often as possible to marvel at nature's beauty and remember its connection to your own.

Seeking Tree Sight

(To heighten intuition)

MATERIALS NEEDED: Twigs, sticks, branches, or other pieces that have fallen from a tree near your home or those in a favored forest

PREPARATION: Collect tree parts that have fallen near your home or in a wooded area—wherever you intend to practice looking from a different vantage. It is best to begin with just one tree and then expand with subsequent casting.

THE WORK:

1. Go before the tree or stand in the central most space of the forest.

2. Take the tree parts and place them in a circle around the tree or under a canopy of multiple trees with yourself inside.

3. Gently rub your hands over the circle in a clockwise motion. Stand and breathe deeply. Raise your arms to the sky and reach as if a tree yourself.

4. Once more, bend down and rub your hands over the circle of tree

parts, but in a clockwise motion.

5. Lay back and press your palms and feet down upon the earth, digging your fingertips and toes in the soil as if rooting yourself.

6. Close your eyes and revel in connecting your energies to the tree(s) before you. Visualize how it "sees" without eyes.

7. Now open your eyes. Slowly stand and reach your arms out at your sides however feels most natural. Allow them to represent your "branches," a conductor of great power and communication for the world around you.

8. Gaze up and focus on the sky. Call upon the trees' nature and the gods' powers to enlighten your perspective.

9. Close your eyes again, but let your senses lead you. See the ground fall away, and your body stretch beyond its flesh confines. Accept any tingling or lightheadedness and look without eyes to the world beneath you. Take in the new air. Sway or hum if the need develops.

10. When exhausted, carefully open your eyes and sit down. Meditate on what you saw.

11. When finished, open the circle and thank the gods.

Spring Awakening

(For renewed energy)

MATERIALS NEEDED: Salt, water, preferred cleansing herb, flowers from blooming tree and common wildflowers

PREPARATION: Gather materials and bring them before the flowering tree. Best done on Ostara or Beltane.

THE WORK:

1. Cast a circle using the salt, water, and cleansing herb, asking the gods to guide your workings.

2. Hold the flowers up to the tree and thank it for its blooms and connection to all wildflowers. Pick up the first bloom and kiss it. Close your eyes and breathe in its fragrance. Let the scent increase your energy. Build your power and let it grow.

3. Now tie the flower to another after kissing it and again taking in the full span of its place in nature.

4. Continue and connect the flowers creating a necklace, wreath, or headpiece while focusing on growing your energies. If pieces break, use others and continue the process.

5. When finished, meditate on the new item. Build your energy by extending the heat within you. Now push all that power into it. See this new craft as an instrument of life, healing, and love.

6. Hang it from the tree and dance in circles singing or chanting the blessings of spring.

7. When exhausted, bow to the tree and retrieve the flower piece. Gift it to someone in need of hope.

Midsummer Sprites

(To boost energy and connect with nature)

MATERIALS NEEDED: Salt, water, preferred cleansing herb, a jar, summer night

PREPARATION: Clean the jar and poke holes in the top. Place grass along the bottom, for it will be temporary for fireflies. Best done on Midsummer or Lammas at twilight.

THE WORK:

1. Cleanse your space by casting a giant circle in a yard, park, or common ground area that houses at least a few trees (a place with a nearby forest is best), using salt, water, and cleansing herb.

2. Reach up to the sky. Focus on the nearest tree line and draw energy from its power by pooling your own personal vibrations and releasing them to it, then calling them back. Greet the gods and all of creation.

3. Then lie down and roll in the grass. Feel the power of their tiny roots beneath you and how all roots reach toward each other.

4. Stand with your jar and walk toward the trees. Go before them with an open heart and eased mind. Step with care and grace, paying attention to all the insects that flit about in the blue sky.

5. As the fireflies awaken, catch one. Just one and hold it in your hands. Bring it as close to your face as possible and watch it fly away.

6. Thank it for gracing you.

7. Now catch more, but place them in the jar. Be sure not to harm them or keep them too long.

8. Once your jar glows with the magic of these wondrous creatures, sit before the jar and hold it in your palms. Close your eyes and feel the light. Feel the jar illuminating with not just a common biological reaction but the elements that drive it, the power that determines all things.

9. Build your energies and visualize yourself lighting up like the bugs before you. Meditate on this magic and let it lead your thoughts.

10. When your ears begin to ring or you grow taxed, open your eyes and gaze upon the lightening bugs once more. Open the lid and set them free. A wave of calm and a rush of air may greet your senses. Marvel in the connection of life and bow to the universe.

Autumnal Tree Divination

(For a better connection with nature and your purpose)

MATERIALS NEEDED: Salt, water, preferred cleansing herb, matches, and a rake

PREPARATION: Best done on Mabon or Samhain. It requires fallen leaves.

THE WORK:

1. Build your energies while raking leaves into a ring at the foot of the tree(s) in your area.

2. Once the ring(s) are complete, go to the nearest tree and place the salt water and cleansing herb before it. Dip your fingers in the water and then the salt. Then rub them on your face and touch the tree.

3. Stand and walk around the tree, stepping on the circle of leaves while dropping the salt to cast a circle. Whisper, chant, or sing to the tree to welcome you.

4. Then turn, take up the water and sanctify the circle with the water, dropping it over the salted leaves. Whisper, chant, or sing asking the tree to accept you as a friend.

5. Stop, grasp the cleansing herb, and light it. Hold it up and around the tree, then wave it down. Whisper, chant, or sing of the eternal bond humans and trees must share.

6. Kneel upon the circle of leaves and press your palms to them. Visualize the power they once held, and how it has been transformed to nourish the remaining life from whence it came.

7. Now press your hands to the tree trunk and open your senses. Medi-

tate on the tree's energy. Extend your power from your core through your own limbs and let them mingle with the tree.

8. When exhausted, open the circle and turn to face the world. Repeat with surrounding trees if possible, then rest your back against the last wooden giant, look out and ground yourself.

Winter Sleep

(To spread good cheer)

MATERIALS NEEDED: Bowl of snow or cold earth, natural decorations ex: sting of popcorn, holly berries, cookies, pinecone bird feeders—made by rolling pinecones in peanut butter and then bird seed for the winter birds, etc.

PREPARATION: Create decorations for the trees in your area as a gift for Yule or Imbolc. Best done with friends and/or family. It is extremely enlightening if each person hosts one tree.

THE WORK:

1. Take items before the nearest tree in the yard and bow before it. Hold up the bowl of snow or cold dirt and thank the gods for providing during the coldest, darkest times.

2. Take up a handful of snow or cold earth and compact it in your palm. Close your eyes and feel its natural power. Build your energies and absorb that of the element in your hand. Then anoint the tree with it, whispering, chanting, or singing to the tree of what beautiful rest offers during winter.

3. Now sit before the tree and hold the decorations one at a time.

Individually charge them with your warmth and love, pooling your energies and pushing the vibrations of your spirit into your creations.

4. Stand and decorate the tree with thought and care. Blanket it like a parent pulling the covers over their child. Sing, chant, or whisper of slowing down to appreciate the season.

5. When finished, bow to the tree and ground.

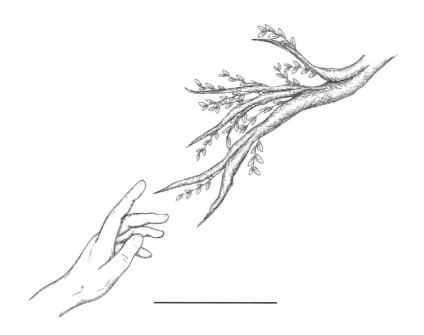

TENDING TREES

TENDING TREES IS REMARKABLE WORK. INDOOR TREES ARE a challenge for those living in apartments or small dwellings. They need the proper sunshine, fresh air, and care that all great plants do. For those caring for land around their home, sometimes it is a matter of protection and survival.

Sick trees or unruly limbs fall. They break off during wind gusts and host the power to do a lot of damage in intense storms.

Just months after I bought my house, a tornado swept through the area. It is not a common event, and I am accustomed to enjoying the fury of a great thunderstorm. My stepson and I played guitar together as my young son sat on the floor playing with his toys. The day was clear, and nothing was forecasted. Out of nowhere, I glanced out the window and watched as a giant branch whipped by.

It was like a cartoon. My stepson and I laughed, but as the winds carried on, I said, "Maybe we should head downstairs." The basement is unfinished but an excellent little shelter; he thought that was a good idea. I grabbed the baby, and we all headed for cover.

The second we got to safety, a great thump shook the house. We waited until the fury of the storm calmed, then went back up to see what had happened. The closest tree to our house had been uprooted and dropped on the corner of the roof right next to where my son had been playing. I've survived many things in life, but this was a new experience.

An overwhelming energy of gratitude filled me. Both boys could have been severely harmed, and each was unscathed. I thanked the gods even as I walked my property and found the backyard flooded like a lake.

My veggie garden was soaked. Everything drowned in that storm except my green beans. I considered the loss a welcome sacrifice compared to what could have happened.

We had been warned about the tree that fell. It was choked to death by fifty-year-old poison ivy vines (I clearly have a thing for fixer-uppers). Somehow this gigantic elm had landed in just the right spot to not break through the house. The roof needed some work, and it took forever to chop the limbs and get the trunk down, but no internal damage affected our home life.

When connecting with trees on a deeper level, one must learn how to protect their life source, spot and treat illnesses, and know when it is time to put one of these wooden giants to rest. A precious relationship develops between my family and the trees we genuinely care for. A bond formed that links us so strongly that we mourned the loss of the tree even though it had been a hazard. There are meditations, rituals, and spells to help homeowners and landowners properly care for trees and assess potentially harmful situations. They have guided my family and me to better care for the space we occupy.

7

TREE HEALING/
RESTING
MEDITATIONS

A TREE'S LIFE (AND SOMETIMES DEATH) HOSTS THE POTENTIAL to spark energies connected to humanity. Like humans (and everything else), trees get sick. Sometimes they recover, and sometimes they die.

There are some instances where damage can create power. In my childhood, I became fascinated by a landmark of sorts in my neighborhood. Down the winding sidewalk that turned away from the brick apartment building I lived in, across a bridge that led over my favorite creek, which flowed just high enough to allow for the perfect explorations to search for crawdads, arrowheads, and stray cats was a field that held a mystical tree.

Whoever said, "lightning never strikes the same place twice," never went there. It was a skinny twisted river birch that stood alone like a lightning rod. Its bark no longer peeled, and many people said it was dead, but its blackened trunk always captivated me.

The air surrounding the strange tree held a pool-like static. Just touching the lines and grooves left behind by the numerous lightning strikes gave me a sense of something greater than myself and modern existence. Standing in its presence alone held power. The mind relaxed and heard distant messages being cast throughout the land.

It had been struck 8 or 9 times when I first walked toward it with my sister. When we moved away, it was up to 11 or 12, but even just thinking of that tree puts my mind in another state.

Some developers bought the land and eventually had it cut down, yet its presence stays with me. I can better visualize the past and look to the future when I recall its image.

I did not know it as a child, but when I sat or stood by that river birch for endless amounts of time, I was meditating. The tree essentially spoke to my instincts and tapped into my subconscious mind. It opened up aspects of my being that I didn't even know existed until I came to it.

Those moments of meditation are not to be overlooked. When a dying or dead tree calls upon us, we must listen. Like a venerable grandparent, it is passing on knowledge and wisdom before it is gone. I always wished to heal that old tree, but it had accepted its fate.

Some meditations offer better insight into how to heal a tree or the self. Others utilize the forces of rest that death, or the coming death, of a great wooden giant can instigate. Throughout my life, river birches have become a nostalgic symbol of change. They were abundant in my neighborhood. My friends and I called them "bacon trees" and played house around them, utilizing the peeling bark as pretend food, paper to write on if we wished to send messages, and sometimes we tossed handfuls into the air as make-believe "snow bark."

No matter what season came, it was "the lightning tree" that gave me a broader sense of how close life is to death. Those energies are linked to such a degree that these simple meditations can be life-changing.

Feeling the Wound

(To aid an injured tree)

Step 1: Go before the tree and close your eyes. Breathe deep. Open all your senses. Focus on the energy of the tree.

Step 2: Open your eyes and examine the injured area. Run your fingers over whatever cuts, bumps, or growths indicate the ailment. Depending on the severity, it may be necessary to remove fungus or mold to better see hallows or grub infestations.

Step 3: Kneel before the roots and place your palms where the trunk meets the earth. Center your thoughts on communicating with the tree's power source. Listen and wait patiently. A sensation of understanding will come in time, better aiding you to sense how quickly treatment or removal will be needed.

Step 4: Once filled with a stronger sense of truth, end meditation and bow to the tree.

Assessing the Air

(To increase awareness of an injured tree's need)

Step 1: Walk up to the tree with a clear head.

Step 2: Circle around it slowly, controlling your breaths. Let the energy build as you go around.

Step 3: Now turn and circle around the tree in the opposite direction, again working to tap into your power and extend it beyond yourself. d.

Step 4: Now sit in front of the tree facing the sun. Close your eyes. Allow all your senses to test the air surrounding the tree as you focus on the energy it omits.

Step 5: Be patient. Mentally see yourself as a neighboring tree. How does the injured bark's aura affect you?

Step 6: Explore what came to you in thought. Then end the meditation and bow to the tree.

Hearing the Call

(To determine whether to heal an injured tree or let it go)

Step 1: Stand as close to the ailing part of the tree as possible.

Step 2: Place your palm on the injured area or as close as possible. Close your eyes and meditate on the wound.

Step 3: Slid your hands down the trunk and to the roots. Sit and focus on connecting with the tree's energies. Feel them out. What do they say?

Step 4: Work to sense growth and healing, or complete losses.

Step 5: Give the great wood time to offer up its truths. Maintain control over yourself and ask the tree if it can reach more or if it is done climbing. Be patient. Fully work to comprehend what is best for the situation. Then end the meditation and bow to the tree.

Finding the Healer Within

(To heal an ailing tree)

Step 1: When it is determined that a tree can be healed, you must draw those powers forth. Connecting with the subject of the change needed is most important. Every day for at least 3 days, sit with the tree, facing the sun and dawn and then again at dusk.

Step 2: As the sun rises or falls, place one hand on the trunk and hold the other palm upward.

Step 3: Draw in the power of the sun. Ask it to guide you, aid you, and increase your abilities, so you can better assist the tree.

Step 4: Focus on honing your energies and your inner light. Practice building that great electricity as you sit with the tree and feel the life before you.

Step 5: Once pushed past the height of your power, slowly relax and end the meditation. Bow to the tree.

Recharging the Tree

(For aiding growth after healing a tree)

Step 1: Stand before the tree facing the sun at sunrise every morning for at least a week. Breathe in, raise your arms, and then breathe out and lower your arms to your sides.

Step 2: Kneel and place your palms at the roots and close your eyes.

Step 3: Extend your energies from your core through your hands, utilizing the extra charge from the sun.

Step 4: Focus on combining the heat of the great gods with yours and the tree's energies to restore health and growth.

Step 5: Visualize the ailment being remedied. Let your mind see the potential for closed wounds, healed bark, or removed parasites

Step 6: Slowly stand and raise your arms to the sky. End the meditation and bow to the tree.

Sealing Your Connection

(To offer healing tree protection and strength)

Step 1: Sit at the tree's roots with your back resting against the trunk facing the sun. Place your hands on the ground at your sides.

Step 2: Close your eyes and pool your energies at your core/center. Feel the warmth inside you and let that heat expand like a ball of electricity.

Step 3: Extend those energies from your body to the roots beneath you. Send out an aura of healing light filled with peace and care.

Step 4:Now clear your mind and draw the energies of the roots toward you. Call to them with your inner being. Ask the tree to work with you so you can aid it in ritual and or spellwork.

Step 5: Mix your power with the tree's. Allow the flowing electricity to mingle and strengthen.

Step 6: During this process, feel out what the tree needs. Also, ponder the physical elements necessary to seal a continued future. Visualize the healing ritual and/or spellwork that is to come.

Step 7: Relax and drawback. End the meditation and bow to the tree.

Bidding Farewell

(To be done when mourning the impending death of an ailing tree)

Step 1: Bow to the tree.

Step 2: Walk to its injury and hold hands over the spot, but not touching it.

Step 3: Build your energies. Let your inner heat grow and expand. Focus on a sensation of cold air or chill to offer soothing ease to the dying or dead tree. Push that numbing aid out.

Step 4: Internally allow your sorrow for the death to be expressed but also your gratitude to the tree, whether through chanting mentally or focusing on a particular image, sensation, or thought.

Step 5: Now, rest your hands on the bark. Rub them over the tree's wounds as best you can. Offer energies of respect and encouragement for the tree's journey to move beyond this life. Say your goodbyes.

Honoring the Ground

(To find peace with death)

Step 1: Walk the land around a dying/dead tree. Then turn and walk around it in the opposite direction.

Step 2: Now, sit down, facing away from the sun, and touch the soil that raised the tree.

Step 3: Close your eyes and clear your mind. Let the energy of the earth fill you. Open your senses.

Step 4: Feel the tree's energy. Think of its past, present, and future. Visualize its life from rooting to what is ahead.

Step 5: Think of life and death. Accept the end that is to come. Explore all thoughts and questions that surface when focusing on mortality.

Step 6: Let your inner strength build. Look beyond time and physical constraints. Think of the heat within and how that energy build and transfers, how it can move on. Images, words, or sensations may come to offer a greater understanding. Offer as much time as possible for spiritual exploration and expansion.

Step 7: When exhausted, slowly draw back your energies. Open your eyes. Bow to the earth and stand. Breathe deep, reach for the sky, exhale, and bring your arms down to your sides.

Uprooting the Voice

(To honor a fallen tree)

Step 1: Once a tree has been removed, go where it once stood.

Step 2: Circle the space. Then turn and circle back, building your energies.

Step 3: Walk to the center where the trunk once held steady. Sit where the tree once stood, facing north (either on the remaining stump, atop the roots, or on the ground where everything has been ground down).

Step 4: Place one hand palm down on the dirt, the other upward toward the sky.

Step 5: Focus your mind on your personal experiences that involve the tree. Even if it was just a pretty sight in the background of life, that is to be remembered.

Step 6: Slowly look to your left. Absorb the scenery and allow your mind to fixate on it. Repeat to the right. Study the view straight down with the same patience and energy, then do the same up above. Feel the elements flowing through the space. The wind, the sunlight, new growth.

Step 7: Stand and face south. Visualize how nature will continue its cycle. Mentally extend your energies and thank the gods for allowing you to live alongside the tree during the last of its life.

Step 8: Bow to the space and walk into the future.

8

———

TREE HEALING/
RESTING RITUALS

ALL THROUGHOUT MY LIFE, I HAVE BONDED WITH certain trees. Some stand strong for me to return to throughout the different phases. Unfortunately, others have been cut down too soon or destroyed over time.

There is a sense of loss when a great giant comes down. My favorite childhood climbing tree was destroyed without a chance to say goodbye. I moved away, and when returning to the area years later, I found nothing but the remnants of a stump. The previously mentioned lightning tree was removed in much the same fashion.

When a tornado brought down a tree on my house, it was sudden and unexpected, but I could at least offer my love to it before it was removed. I found peace in ritual and acceptance in returning the wood to the earth.

Just as healing powers forge growth, there is a similar aspect to letting go. The following rituals offer up both options in their own rites.

Clearing the Air

(To purify a natural tree space for balance)

MATERIALS NEEDED: Matches and preferred cleansing herb
PREPARATION: Do after connecting to a tree through meditation. Preferably during a waning moon.

THE WORK:

1. Stand before the tree and raise your arms to the limbs. Chant, sing, or whisper of the importance it has held.

2. Lower your arms to your sides and bow your head. Pool your energies until your body feels fully charged.

3. Then light the cleansing herb and hold it out. Circle the tree trunk while holding the cleansing herb and chant, sing, or whisper words, allowing the surrounding energies to step back and let the energy flow freely.

4. Turn and bend toward the roots, circling the tree in the opposite direction. Again chant, sing, or whisper to push the current energies away to give the tree space for healing or death.

5. Once more, turn and hold the cleansing herb up (careful not to hit any limbs or leaves) and circle the tree one last time while chanting, singing, or whispering for the air to clear to allow the future through.

6. Then stand before the tree facing the sun. Wave the cleansing herb in a circle before yourself, and thank the gods for your part in this fate.

Healing the Lengths

(To heal a tree from root to canopy-best for when parasite or illness has taken hold)

MATERIALS NEEDED: Stick from the tree, lavender flowers, oil, and/or incense, and garden shovel (if using lavender plant)
PREPARATION: Meditate on the stick. Build your energies and extend them into the stick. Best done during the full moon period.

THE WORK:

1. Place the lavender at the root of the tree. (If using incense, light it now.) Tap the tip of the stick on the flowers, in the oil, and/or around the incense.

2. Kneel before the tree and close your eyes. Let your inner powers build until they flow from you. Push them through your arm, down your hands, fingers, and into the stick, visualizing the energy as a healing light.

3. Direct the stick at the roots of the tree and focus on sending that light to the roots of the tree in need.

4. Whisper, chant, or sing of warding off all ailments. See healthy, strong roots in your mind. Let those images inspire words for you to chant, sing, or whisper to the tree.

5. Breathe deep and stand. Repeat this process for the trunk, first tapping the tip of the stick on the flowers, in the oil, and/or around the incense.

6. Gaze up to the limbs. One last time, tap the tip of your stick on the flowers, in the oil, and/or around the incense, then repeat the process by holding the stick up for the limbs. You may wish to climb into the

boughs for a stronger connection.

7. Now take up the incense and walk around the tree. Anoint whatever branches and limbs you can reach, or/then bury the lavender at the foot of the tree between the roots asking the Gods for aid.

Damage Control

(To heal small/specific area ailing a tree)

MATERIALS NEEDED: Honey and lavender oil or flowers

PREPARATION: Mix the lavender into the honey, then meditate on it, pouring all your healing energies into the mixture to create a salve. Best done during the full moon period.

THE WORK:

1. Go before the tree and hold up the salve. Chant, sing, or whisper of working to heal.

2. Ask the Gods for aid and go to the area that needs aid.

3. Dip fingers into the salve and gently brush onto the affected area. Coat on thickly. It's okay if it drips so long as the area is properly covered.

4. Once coated, face the sun and place your palms on the trunk in front of you. Close your eyes and visualize the tree healing. Push your energies into the trunk and through the tree around its wound.

5. Bow for the work and look to the future with hope. Meditate on this purpose daily, thinking of the salve and the power you hold for the next week.

Regular Upkeep

MATERIALS NEEDED: Matches and preferred cleansing herb-
PREPARATION: Meditate to connect with the tree. Best done during the waxing moon phase.

THE WORK:

1. Light cleansing herb and hold out to the tree. Walk in a circle around the trunk, bringing the cleansing herb up and down to cleanse the area all over. Turn and repeat in the opposite direction.
2. Stand before the tree facing the sun. Hold cleansing herb before you and close your eyes. Visualize yourself as a tree. Let your energies root at your center and spread through your being as the smoke curls.
3. Focus on extending your healing power from the warmth at your core, through your feet, and into the earth before you. Push these "roots" to mingle with those of the tree and recharge them with vitality and life.
4. Chant, sing, or whisper of your purpose and the tree's future.
5. Ask the Gods to hear this call. Bow to the tree and walk on. Do this as many times as needed during the healing process.

Accepting Fate

(Ritual to honor the tree and prepare it for rest)

MATERIALS NEEDED: Sticks and flowers

PREPARATION: Gather sticks fallen from the dying tree and place them in a circle around its base. Then pick flowers (preferably from your garden or ones that grow wild nearby) and scatter them within the circle of sticks. Meditate on the sticks and flowers, offering hopeful energy.

THE WORK:

1. Decorate the branches with flowers. Stand the sticks up against the trunk in a circle.

2. Bow to the tree gazing upon its roots, facing the sun. As you stand to full height again, allow your eyes to follow the length of the trunk, then look up to the limbs above. Breathe deep and raise your arms to them.

3. Chant, sing, or whisper thanks to the great wooden giant for all it has offered you.

4. Now step facing away from the sun. Chant, sing, or whisper thanks for this tree's importance to the insects, animals, and other plants nearby.

5. Lower your arms, place your palms upon the trunk, and look up the great length. Breathe deep. Feel your love toward the tree and its place in existence.

6. Bow to the tree and thank it for being a part of life.

Respectful Lie Down

(For when a tree is cut down)

MATERIALS NEEDED: Fallen tree, matches, and 3 white candles (carved with images of the tree's seed, fully grown, and its spirit)

PREPARATION: Meditate on the candles as symbols and neutral guides for what is to come. Do it as soon after the tree is cut as possible.

THE WORK:

1. Set the candles in the center of the downed tree.

2. Bow to the tree and chant, sing, or whisper of the fall that comes for everything.

3. Breathe deep and raise your arms up. Looking to the sky, chant, sing, or whisper for the Gods to honor this rite with you.

4. Now, light the seed candle, and speak of the tree's youth.

5. Then, light the adult tree candle, speaking of the tree's life and strength.

6. Last, light the spirit candle and speak of the energies of life that flow to the Gods.

7. Kneel before the candles and focus on them. Let your energies extend beyond yourself to the trees and your creator(s).

8. When exhausted, relax and let the candles burn down.

Honoring the Heights

(To remember your connection to a fallen tree)

MATERIALS NEEDED: Sticks and flowers

PREPARATION: Collect sticks from the tree. Pick flowers (from your garden or the wild nearby). Meditate on them to honor the tree, which is no more. Place the sticks in a circle around the stump or where the tree once stood. Then sprinkle the flowers inside the barrier closer to the roots and trunk.

THE WORK:

1. Walk around the circle recalling all the memories of its presence in your life.

2. Turn and circle the space in the opposite direction focusing on the countless insects, animals, and other plants it must have influenced.

3. Now step into the circle. Walk upon the flower petals and visualize the tree's spirit resting.

4. Turn and walk in the opposite direction, focusing on the energy it carries into the unknown. Connect with that power.

5. Sit in the center where the tree once lived (upon the stump if needed). Chant, sing, or whisper your thanks to the tree and the universe for its purpose.

Soothing the Stump

(Ritual for stump grinding)

MATERIALS NEEDED: Stick from the removed tree
PREPARATION: Meditate on the stick to connect your energies to it. Do this on the morning before the stump removal.

THE WORK:
1. Go before the stump facing away from the sun. Hold the stick over it and chant, sing, or whisper your sympathies for what remains.
2. Build your energies. Walk around the stump, directing the end of the stick at it while focusing on offering calming power.
3. Turn and walk in the opposite direction, pushing out soothing love.
4. Tap the stump at the four corners and call upon the gods, asking them to be present for the transition.
5. Bow to the stump and turn away.

Remembering the Being

(Root grinding ceremony)

MATERIALS NEEDED: Stick from the fallen tree, a handful of surrounding dirt, and an optional garden shovel if the ground is hard.
PREPARATION: Meditate on the stick as a symbol of the tree's spirit. Do the morning of the grinding.

THE WORK:

1. Go before the remaining roots, place the stick in the earth before them, and stand it up in the soil.

2. Visualize the tree that once was. Focus on what it meant to you, and let that journey guide you through its greater meaning.

3. Take up the handful of dirt and walk around the roots with it in hand, building your energies. Push that power into the soil with hopes for the future.

4. Then kneel before the stick, carefully set the dirt around it, and pack the earth around it as a memorial.

5. Turn in the opposite direction you walked before and walk or dance around the roots chanting, singing, or whispering of remembrance. Thank the gods for the time offered, and look to the future with hope.

9

TREE HEALING/
RESTING SPELLS

E VEN FALLEN TREES CONTAIN AN AURA OF GREATNESS. Long trunks lying in forest scenes host new powers. They become hollows for creatures, and the world continues growing around them, absorbing them into their bosom.

I adore encountering overgrown remnants. Sitting upon the mossy seat of a downed tree provides insight. It is a great place to build energies or decorate a natural altar for spellwork. There are times when utilizing the space of a rested tree for the sake of healing another grants us the added power to fully realize our potential.

Everything is connected. How we approach meditation, ritual, and lead into spellwork is intertwined like the roots that mingle far beneath our feet.

No loss should ever be viewed as a failure. All lives have their turn and demise. Working to aid an ailing tree or others may not always bring about the desired outcome, but each experience can teach us how to improve our relationships with ourselves, nature, and the Gods.

Tree Healing/Resting Spells combine all aspects of being to either influence or ease what can be survived and what cannot. They are made of more than just wood. Like all spiritual connections, these spells hold answers for many other forms of life.

Soothing the Site

(A spell to ease tree wounds or surrounding areas)

MATERIALS NEEDED: Salt, water, matches, preferred cleansing herb, fire-safe plate or bowl, honey, lavender (flowers or ground up), cinnamon

PREPARATION: Bless the salt and water. Mix the honey, lavender, and cinnamon to create a salve. Measure as you need with ample cinnamon. Meditate on it, pouring all your healing powers into the concoction. Best done on the waxing moon cycle or the full moon at night.

THE WORK:

1. Place materials at the foot of the tree. Bow to the wooden giant. Then examine the affected area(s).

2. Light the cleansing herb and walk around the tree, carefully waving the herb around to cleanse the space. Stop before the wound. Hold it over the injury/ailment and chant, sing, or whisper for the universe to offer its healing aid. Place the herb on/in the fireproof plate/bowl as close to the area as possible and let it burn.

3. Take up the salt and turn, sprinkling it as you walk around the tree chanting, singing, or whispering for the powers of the elements to protect you in your workings.

4. Put the salt down and take up the water. Turn and sprinkle the water in the opposite direction you laid down the salt. Chant, sing, or whisper for the powers of the elements to seal your work with their light of the Gods.

5. Return the water and take up the salve. Hold it up to the sky.

Commune with the moon, letting the light pour down on you and the tree. Let those energies draw out your power. Grow it until your hands feel electrified.

6. Now coat your hands in the salve and gently rub the broken area of the tree. As you do so, visualize the injury or ailment healing, that area of bark sealing itself off from the tree so the rest of it can grow safely.

7. When fully covered, step back and rub your hands at the tree's base on the ground by the roots. Kneel and chant, sing, or whisper your purpose, pushing out the need for growth after pain.

8. Then stand and open the circle.

Structural Support Spell

(Cast when needing to offer aid for reconstructive tree growth all around)

MATERIALS NEEDED: Salt, water, matches, preferred cleansing herb, fire-safe plate or bowl, 2 large branches (that have fallen from another tree) or planks of wood, milk (for feeding the tree), and cinnamon (enough to darken milk).

PREPARATION: Bless the salt and water. Mix the milk and cinnamon while meditating on your purpose. Pour healing energy into the liquid. Then charge the branches or planks with the powers of strength and support. Best done during a waxing moon or on the full moon at night

THE WORK:

1. Stand the fallen branches or planks up against either side of the tree facing the moon. Set the other materials at the foot of the tree. Bow to the wooden giant. Then go beneath the boughs placing palms on the trunk, and gaze up. Close your eyes and connect with the tree's spirit.

2. Light the cleansing herb and walk around the tree, carefully moving the burning plant up and down to cleanse the entire area. Reach up and slowly bring the cleansing herb from your highest reach down to the earth and chant, sing, or whisper for the Gods to offer their healing aid. Place the herb on/in the fireproof plate/bowl at the foot of the tree.

3. Take the salt and turn, sprinkling it as you walk around the tree in the opposite direction as before. Chant, sing, or whisper for the powers of the elements to protect you in your workings.

4. Put the salt down and take up the water. Turn and sprinkle the water in the opposite direction you laid down the salt. Chant, sing, or whisper for the powers of the elements to seal your work with their guidance by the power of the Gods.

5. Stand between the planks and reach one arm toward each. Let the electricity within build and extend to the supports. Visualize them aiding the healing process, offering a new phase of life for the great trunk.

6. Now take the mixture. Pour a few drops over each support, chanting, singing, or whispering for them to stand strong.

7. Then kneel before the roots of the tree. Gaze up at the moon. Let its light charge you, allow you to see and feel beyond yourself. Slowly feed the tree the mixture, gently pouring it over the roots at the base. Chant, sing, or whisper of healing and life.

8. Breathe deep and draw yourself back. Stand up and break the circle.

Limb Healing Spell

(To be cast when a single tree limb is ailing)

MATERIALS NEEDED: Salt, water, matches, preferred cleansing herb, fire-safe plate or bowl, honey, cinnamon, garden shovel, a handful of dirt

PREPARATION: Bless the salt and water. Best done during a full moon or waxing cycle.

THE WORK:

1. Bring materials and place them at the foot of the tree. Look over the broken or ailing limb.

2. Cast a circle, clearing the space with the cleansing herb while chanting for the universe's blessing while walking around the tree. Turn and walk while spilling the salt as you ask for focus. Do the same with the water, then stand within your space facing the moon.

3. Now take up the honey and build your energies. Focus on healing power. Extend it beyond yourself into the liquid. Then pour it over the break/injury site, chanting, singing, or whispering of healing aid.

4. Now move on to the cinnamon. As before, focus on the healing energy needed to aid the limb. Push it into the helpful spice, then slowly scatter it over the honey, covering all of it.

5. Grab the garden shovel and kneel before the tree. Look to the sky and let the moon's light empower you. Dig up enough dirt to pack into the wound over the honey and cinnamon. Rise up, and handful by handful, do the deed while chanting, singing, or whispering of the purpose—to seal the injury with the healing power of the honey and cinnamon inside.

6. When fully covered, raise arms to the treetops. Sway or dance around the tree as you feel moved to do. Let your inner electricity build and build until you feel ready to burst. Then direct hands toward the limb in need and visualize healing power radiating from yourself into the tree.

7. Step back and breathe deeply. Bow to the tree and thank the Gods. Open the circle and ground yourself.

Trunk Healing Spell

(To restore health to a favorite tree's trunk)

MATERIALS NEEDED: Salt, water, matches, preferred cleansing herb, fire-safe plate or bowl, lemon juice, honey, lavender (flowers or oil)

PREPARATION: Bless the salt and water. Best done during a full moon or waxing cycle.

THE WORK:

1. Bring materials and place them at the foot of the tree. Rub your hands over the trunk.

2. Cast a circle, clearing the space with the cleansing herb while chanting for the Gods' blessing as you walk around the tree. Turn and walk around, spilling the salt as you focus on the element's power. Do the same with the water, then stand within your space facing the moon.

3. Now take up the lemon juice and build your energies. Focus on cleansing the tree. Breathe in the natural aid. Let the aroma conse-

crate the space.

4. Then hold the honey in its container. Build your energies and pour them into the thick liquid.

5. Grab the lavender and crush or drop into the honey while chanting, singing, or whispering of healing the trunk's ailment. If bark is broken, remove the rotten pieces.

6. Brush fingers into the mixture and paint the ailing trunk area(s) with the newly created mixture.

7. Stoop to the ground and wipe your hands at the tree's base. Then draw your palms together and bow to the tree. Raise your arms up to the highest reaches and let the moon guide you.

8. Sway, move, or dance around the tree until you feel fully recharged, then place your hands on the trunk and direct that electricity into your purpose, calling on the aid of the Gods.

9. Breathe deep and slowly draw back. Bow to the tree and offer it words of hope. Thank the Gods.

Root Protection

(Spell to aid roots against grubs and parasites)

MATERIALS NEEDED: Salt, water, matches, preferred cleansing herb, fire-safe plate or bowl, garden shovel, garlic, lemon juice, diatomaceous earth

PREPARATION: Bless the salt and water. Best done during a full moon or waxing cycle.

THE WORK:

1. Take materials to the foot of the tree. Kneel before the roots and place your hands on the ground. Feel the energies/ailments affecting the energies of the space below.

2. Cast a circle, clearing the area with the cleansing herb. Walk around the tree, chanting for the universe's blessing.

3. Grab the salt and turn. Walk an opposite circle, spilling the salt and focusing on its power of neutrality.

4. Now turn again and take up the water repeating this circular walk and spilling the water around the circle.

5. Then kneel facing the moon.

6. Grasp the shovel and gently dig a small layer of dirt off the roots all the way around. Chant, sing, or whisper your purpose to comfort the tree and ask for the universe's aid.

7. Take the garlic and pour a generous coating over the lightly unearthed roots. Focus on cleansing the area and warding off pests/ailments. Chant, sing, or whisper of banishing all ills.

8. Bring the lemon juice before you. Dip your fingertips into it. Pour healing energy into this cleansing liquid. Then slowly pour it over the bare roots all around the trunk.

9. Finally, take the diatomaceous earth. Hold it up to the moon, letting the light charge it. Stand and sprinkle it over the roots in a thick coating of powder. Chant, sing, or whisper for the tree to grow healthy and live well.

10. Kneel once more and push the dirt over the roots, packing it to seal the area.

11. Sit back and hold your arms to the sky. Thank the Gods for aiding this work. Open the circle and ground yourself.

Drawing Down Wisdom

(Spell to absorb knowledge from a tree before it comes down)

MATERIALS NEEDED: Salt, water, matches, preferred cleansing herb, garden shovel, a candle (with an image of the spirit carved into the wax), a journal, and a pen

PREPARATION: Bless the salt and water. Perform on a full moon

THE WORK:

1. Go before the tree. Dig a little space to hold the candle in the ground at its base and set the candle in the dirt.

2. Stand and look to the moon. Let the light illuminate your spirit.

3. Cast a circle, clearing the space with the cleansing herb while walking around the tree, chanting for the universe's blessing. Turn and grab salt spilling it as you focus on the neutral power while you walk another circle. Turn one last time and do the same with the water.

4. Kneel before the tree, chanting, singing, or whispering for it to share its great understanding with you.

5. Light the candle and focus your energies on the flame. Let them flow.

6. Open your senses. See more than just what is before you. Listen to the electricity around the tree. Feel what is true.

7. Sit comfortably and grab the pen and paper. Write what comes to you. The words will come as they need.

8. Do this until the candle burns out.

9. When extinguished, read the passages out loud. Then bow to the tree and thank it for all you have learned.

Falling Tree Spell

(*Spell to aid a tree and its space in rest*)

MATERIALS NEEDED: Salt, water, matches, preferred cleansing herb, fireproof container, garden shovel, freshly picked flowers (preferably from the area)

PREPARATION: Bless the salt and water. Best done the night after the tree is cut down. If in control of when the tree is laid down, a waxing cycle is best.

THE WORK:

1. Place your materials on the fallen trunk.

2. Walk around the entire tree, looking over its extensive greatness. Feel the energies surrounding it and let your inner warmth build, expand, and mingle with that air.

3. Light the cleansing herb and wave it over the tree from end to end. Leave it to burn in/on a fireproof container.

4. Cast a circle with the salt and water, first walking in one direction, spilling the salt, and calling on the Gods to be closer, then walking in the opposite direction with the water, dropping it over the salt with words welcoming the elements.

5. Take up the shovel and kneel before the tree. Dig up the earth, gathering as much soil as possible. Fill both hands and hold them up to the night sky. Chant, sing, or whisper of going back from whence we came and resting peacefully in the dirt that bore us. Stand and slowly scatter the dirt on as much of the trunk as possible.

6. Grasp the flowers. Hold them up to the sky and breathe in. Focus

your energies on life and death's dance; their marriage.

7. Slowly break off the stems and carefully scatter the blooms over the trunk where the dirt has fallen.

8. Stand before the trunk. Close your eyes and focus on aiding the tree in its new rest. Then bow to it and open the circle. A small feast may be served afterward.

Honoring the Reach

(To be done after a tree is removed and the earth has healed)

MATERIALS NEEDED: Salt, water, matches, preferred cleansing herb, fireproof container, stick from the tree, garden shovel

PREPARATION: Bless the salt and water.

THE WORK:

1. Walk through the newly cleared space and place the materials at the center. (If stump remains, make that your altar).

2. Cleanse the space with the cleansing herb, asking for the universe to aid you. Put it out in the fireproof container.

3. Cast a circle, spilling the salt while chanting, singing, or whispering of the elemental powers before you. Then turn and seal it by dropping the water on the salt as you walk in the opposite direction, chanting, singing, or whispering of sealing the space for your workings.

4. Take up the stick and hold it to the sky. Visualize the tree that once reached above, the energy and force that took. Let the stick absorb all

of that electricity.

5. Dance around the space, building your own power. Let your spirit reach far beyond yourself.

6. Then take the garden shovel and bend down to the earth. Dig a small hole and set the stick in it, standing up like a tree. Pack the dirt around the base, so it remains upright.

7. Once more, dance around the stick, extending your energies to honor the life that was and your own life that continues. Thank the gods for all you are and your connection to all the living creatures you meet.

8. When exhausted, bow to the little stick, remembering the heights it once knew. Open the circle and walk with purpose.

Eternal Growth Spell

(To accept life and death with love and comfort)

MATERIALS NEEDED: Salt, water, matches, candle (carved with the tree's former image), dagger, and stick from the tree

PREPARATION: Set a small altar in your home. Place the salt to the left (west), the water to the right (east), the candle in the center, the stick at the top (north), and the dagger nearest to you at the bottom (south). Bless the water and salt.

THE WORK:

1. Stand before the altar. Cast a circle with salt and water, acknowledging the elements in the gods' name.

2. Take up the dagger and point it above you, chanting, singing, or whispering for the realm above to meet you. Then point the dagger down to the ground, chanting, singing, or whispering for the realm below to meet you.

3. Kneel before the altar and light the candle speaking of the eternal growth that lives in all bonds of existence. Focus on the flame's light and visualize the removed tree. Call its energies to you.

4. Draw forth your power and see yourself growing as the tree did and dying as well. Cast all fear from your heart and look beyond the ending of this singular life. Let the tree's spirit aid you on this journey of looking further.

5. When exhausted, take up the stick. Hold it above the flame (at a safe distance) and consecrate the remnants as a symbol of vitality.

6. Use the dagger to carve a pattern or image into the stick. Upon finishing the design leave the stick to lie before the candle until it burns out. Set it aside for use in the future when needing guidance.

7. Stand and raise arms up, then extend them down. Thank the tree and all of creation for being present with you as you explore the waking world in this life.

8. Then break the circle and ground yourself.

EMPOWERING TREE MAGIC

NO MATTER HOW FAST THE WORLD MOVES, PEOPLE will always need trees. Life has significantly changed between my grandmother's time and the modern era. Many spaces have been altered. Housing and businesses have swept the globe, communication has expanded in both reach and quickness, and schedules are much tighter.

There are pros and cons to this. Humanity can balance it all when given proper incentives. We need the energies of the trees and their realms to retain our health and wellness as much as we need each other.

Cities that host spaces for trees and other plants are cleaner and more welcoming. Suburban areas that house parks and nature reserves are in demand. The countryside remains green and alive. Each dwelling area thrives best when reminded of our connection to nature and the great wooden giants that provide the breath of life.

Our world may change drastically in just a decade or two but greeting a tree and feeling its power reminds us of the deeper connections that never die. Time is slow. It becomes easier to breathe and clear one's mind. The mental and physical aspects of being flourish when greenery is present. Strength and power are readily displayed. We live healthier and longer when continuously engaging with trees.

The famously despised mystic, Grigori Efimovich Rasputin, is a perfect example of someone whose power was nurtured by the countryside, trees, and all nature has to offer. A healer, he gained great fame saving lives with his miraculous abilities, but during periods when he became caught up in the lavishness of the Russian royal family and neglected his spiritual connection to the trees and all creatures beyond St. Petersburg, his magic waned, and times grew harsher.

Like many other great mystics, he understood that meditation and ties to the land were godly/universal. When bustling through urban areas, it is easier to forget the trees even if they reach out for you, but the more consumed we become, the more critical these bonds are.

Everyone goes through periods of waxing and waning. My own personal daily mediations are sometimes neglected. During these periods, I am more easily exhausted and frustrated; it becomes difficult to carry on with what is expected of me, and I have to fight to regain that sense of self.

Life shifts, and we must adjust. There is nothing wrong with needing to recharge but falling prey to egotism or the constant desire to help others is unhealthy. All spiritualists need periods of solitude to sort through their learnings. The trees stand tall, awaiting us in these times.

Wisdom is better found in the quiet. Tree meditations dull the noises of society. When unable to venture beyond a populated setting, focus does not take root as easily, making it is even more important. Regularly visiting the trees (or even just one) and performing specific meditations to remain grounded and humble draw the elements closer to us.

When we sense the elements on a higher level, we can walk more freely. During the brief period that I lived alone in Los Angeles, there were dark nights when I trusted the rats and the small city trees to guide me home safely. If they were near, I knew danger was not present. This relaxed me where it may have repelled others but finding ease no matter where I go is a skill I have honed.

Rituals can and should be performed anywhere. Some places are more sacred than others, but the true home is within, and to magnify that truth, a person must explore it first-hand. Turning to the trees in an unknown space provides familiarity. No matter the species, it is connected to the underground network of life. Deeper meanings are found in those spaces I travel when I carry out my rituals as I go because I know that the trees have influenced each movement no matter where I step.

Implementing the meanings and connections built from these experiences heighten powers. Spellwork is more successful when performed by a knowledgeable individual who controls their meditations and rituals and is ready to absorb new purposes and responsibilities. Like the trees that we cannot live without, we must grow strong yet flexible in our practices.

It takes a strong will to continuously grow with the Gods. Plenty of distractions and temptations have led great people down the path of degradation, but the beauty of magic is that no one can fall behind so far that they are beyond redemption. The trees exude this. Even when no longer able to climb, they nourish the land. We can follow this example with grace and dignity no matter where we are.

10

TREE ESCAPE MEDITATIONS

MEDITATION IS OFTEN NEEDED TO ESCAPE MODERN CONFINES. The term escape means many things to society, but in this context, it is purely breaking free and avoiding unwanted outcomes.

Tree escape meditations offer peace from within. There are always instances where we cannot just walk away from crowded places and clear our heads. Like happiness, peace is not a destination but a state of mind one must achieve no matter how tumultuous their situation is.

Running away to the woods always sounds romantic, but more realistically, I have had to look to the trees growing in the forest of my heart to clear my thoughts regularly. As a child, just looking out the window and finding a tree aided me when fearing my father or trying not to cry at school. This has carried well into adulthood. Office work, housework, and yardwork are all better tackled with a calm aspect. Some of the meditations listed here are more involved, but all utilize the same energies to build soothing powers which guide the brain away from mental prisons.

Tree Visualization

(To Slow Down a fast-paced life)

Step 1: Take a deep breath and close your eyes. It doesn't matter where you are or what you're doing, so long as you can take a moment or a few.

Step 2: Think of your favorite tree (or one you have admired recently). Bring the image of it to mind as clear as day.

Step 3: Focus on the branches. See the leaves, twigs, or needles springing from them.

Step 4: Now visualize the grooves of the leaves, twigs, or needles. Let the patterns guide you, relax you. Trace them in your mind's eye.

Step 5: Open your eyes and look at your hands. Examine your fingers and really look at the design of your fingerprints. Think of how they are unique to you, just as tree patterns are markings of natural identity.

Step 6: Breathe deep and carry on.

Window Meditation

(To bring peace)

Step 1: Look to a window with a view of a familiar tree. If needed, go to the window (if unable to see from the current position), or visualize a tree if none sits outside whatever building you feel "trapped" in.

Step 2: LTake a deep breath and gaze upon the great plant. Slowly look from root to branches.

Step 3: Look at your feet, up your legs, and your body.

Step 4: Stare back at the tree and look for movement. Whether by wind or from the movement of creatures, see the rhythm of nature.

Step 5: Now think of your pulse, your breathing; the drumming of your life. Feel the connection. Let it empower you no matter your surroundings.

Step 6: Breathe deep and be calm.

Shifting Peace Meditation

(For Coping with Changes in our environment or life)

Step 1: Go outside. Walk before a tree in the new space or one that is less familiar if still in the same area.

Step 2: Step as close to it as possible, then turn and look at the world facing the sun.

Step 3: Breathe deep. Close your eyes. Open your senses. Smell the bark. Hear the birds and bustling. Feel the energies of nature flow.

Step 4: Visualize life before whatever changes took place. Recall the best and worst aspects of it.

Step 5: Now force yourself to focus on the possibilities of the change, both the negative and positive aspects that bring it into balance.

Step 6: See yourself flourishing through the change and those to come.

Step 7: Open your eyes and take some time to breathe and be free. Then walk with a purpose.

Quieting the Background

(To be done when feeling trapped and unable to leave a space)

Step 1: Breathe deep and hum low to yourself. Focus on the buzzing within, the vibrations of your body.

Step 2: Close your eyes. Visualize your energies as roots connecting you to the area but reaching much further than your body. They may sing with a slight tinkling sound. Let that harmonize with your quiet humming.

Step 3: Listen to your pulse and how it drums within. This internal symphony can tune out anything. Focus on relaxing your physical self while tuning the senses.

Step 4: Now stop humming. Open your eyes. The noises which distracted you before should be lessened, if not unnoticeable.

Step 5: Repeat as many times as needed.

Strengthening Flexibility Inside and Out

(To revive the senses, body, and spirit)

Step 1: Sit or stand erect. Close your eyes and breathe deeply.

Step 2: Visualize yourself as a tree in a storm. Bend to the left, stretching your sides, then to the right. Imagine the wind blowing around you, the inner storm that sometimes rages.

Step 3: Now think of the pains ailing your mind, your body, or the woes stunting your spirit. See them as the dispersing clouds. They are nothing more than passing obstacles.

Step 4: Reach up and clear them away. Now bend down and think of pulling nutrients from the soil beneath you.

Step 5: Once more, sit or stand straight and tall. Inhale slowly. Feel the clear air reviving you. Exhale slowly and let go of any excess tension. Repeat as many times as needed throughout your day.

Shading Dark Thoughts to Bring Light

(To balance yourself and accept that life holds both positive and negative energies for a reason)

Step 1: Go outside and sit in the shade of a tree facing out, leaning your back against the trunk. Relax your eyes and focus on the shadow surrounding you. See how it affects the ground and everything it touches.

Step 2: Let the darkness cover you. See it as a blanket dropped from the tree for comfort.

Step 3: Think of any significant issues that have been interfering with your life. Examine them: the origin, cycles, and meaning.

Step 4: Now gaze at the line where the shadow stops. See how the light washes out the colors beyond. It can be brilliant at times but does not remove anything, just shifts the focus.

Step 5: Breathe deep. Look further. Focus your eyes and visualize a shift inside.

Step 6: Perpetuate that shift by guiding your thoughts toward a new perspective while seeking solutions for any instances that can be dealt with.

Step 7: Stand and thank the tree for its guidance.

The Peace Within

(To bring confidence and peace when making a drastic change for your safety/sanity)

Step 1: Stand or sit tall when unable to walk away from stress or a hostile situation. Breathe deep and bow your head slightly like a tree bracing for a storm.

Step 2: Let the breath fill your body with air and calm your mind and spirit. Let each breath warm your body and expand the heat within. Feel each heartbeat and envision how this pulse sets the rhythm of your future and purpose.

Step 3: If being harmed by an individual, or others, now is the time to stand tall and make your exit with grace and brevity. If facing non-threatening pressures or unrest, visualize the sunset that will come and keep breathing and utilizing your inner strength to maintain your calm.

Step 4: Once past the climax of the situation, visualize your energies growing beyond yourself, sending out comforting electricity for anyone else who may need aid.

Breathing Break

*(When feeling anxious, depressed, or in need of a
spiritual boost)*

Step 1: Go outside. Look to the sky and breathe deeply.

Step 2: Find a tree to gaze at from a distance. Just look at the towering height and how it contrasts with the endless expanse of the horizon.

Step 3: Become conscious of each breath, carefully drawing in oxygen and slowly breathing out CO_2.

Step 4: Close your eyes and envision your energies as a light that flows in and out as you breathe. This light may take on a color or shape. Let it form as needed.

Step 5: Turn your inner eye to the tree ahead and see it taking in your breaths and sending out oxygen as if breathing in the opposite manner of your process. Connect your energies to it and work on visualizing the light of the tree's power flowing in and out in a dance of color and electricity that bonds you together.

Step 6: Relax in this image for as long as necessary. Then open your eyes, bow to the tree, and continue your day with a renewed sense of purpose.

Focused Sight

*(To build focus and confidence in a difficult task or
endeavor)*

Step 1: Sit or stand tall. Look at the task before you.

Step 2: Breathe deep and root yourself to dedicated completion. If needed, chant or repeat a mental message stating the need to focus and finish what is required.

Step 3: Envision your hands as fertilizer working to nourish the intended outcome. Build your energies and mix them with each effort.

Step 4: Let the task root itself in your brain. Keep your sight set on aiding in its growth. Look beyond the present and see the outcome as it will be.

Step 5: Continue this process until either finished or at a stopping point. If needed, repeat until the project/task is completed over a longer period. 10

11

———

TREE RELAXATION/ DEEPER MEANING RITUALS

RITUALS— WHETHER ELABORATE OR HUMBLE, OPEN NEW PATHWAYS to understanding and exploration of our connection with the Gods. Not every ceremony has to be a giant festival. Certain times and places heighten abilities, but when seeking relaxation or deeper meanings, all one needs is a tree, a little time, and maybe a few additional materials to better bridge the unknown with more tangible lessons already learned and put into practice.

For years I have performed small rituals in various places, and they always aid me. Some are subconsciously carried out. Others are more purposeful. I don't always realize the weight of what calls to me until I have engaged the energies, but my instincts guide me, and my purpose is clear. Simple rituals can be carried out in any setting to ease the body and find deeper meanings.

Morning Hopes

(To better focus on meeting daily goals)

MATERIALS NEEDED: A basket, sticks, twigs, leaves, nuts, and a garden shovel

PREPARATION: Take a walk and gather unusual sticks, leaves, or seed pods that have fallen off the trees along your path.

THE WORK:

1. Sit beneath a familiar tree and meditate on the collected items in the basket.

2. One by one, pull each out and focus on one hope/desire for the day.

3. Pool your energies and push them into the item. Repeat as needed for different accomplishments.

4. Now toss each hope/desire before the tree individually, except for the one most dear to you. When releasing each one back upon the ground, visualize yourself obtaining your goals.

5. Take the last hopeful item with you and place it in a visible area of your home or workspace as a reminder of the power within and the connections it holds with the gods.

Lunch Break Realizations

(To connect with nature and your spirituality during a busy workday)

MATERIALS NEEDED: Collected rock(s)

PREPARATION: Dress for the weather or wait for a clear day

THE WORK:

1. Go outside and take a walk during your break. Look to the sky and breathe deeply. Open your senses and remind yourself of the greater energies that exist beyond menial tasks or compensation.

2. Now focus before you. Explore what lies ahead. Be observant and appreciate the contrast between the wide world to the confines of most working atmospheres.

3. Gaze upon the ground before you as you walk. Study the plants and insects working in the area.

4. Now search for a rock or pebbles that speak to you. Ones that catch your eye or harbor a specific aura.

5. Bring it/them along for the rest of the walk. Hold onto your new find(s). Absorb their energies; let the minerals refresh your connection to the wild world.

6. When it is time to return, stop before a familiar tree and place the rock(s) against the trunk. Think of the people who have come into your life for only a part of the journey. Those friends who are there for you and help you get from one point to another seem to fade out of your life as quickly as they entered. Breaks are like that.

7. Smile and look at the tree, how it spans over as much as possible, no matter how big or small. Bow to it and go back to your tasks refreshed.

Evening Teachings

(To be done at the end of a long day for relaxation and stress reduction)

MATERIALS NEEDED: Paper, crayon or pencil, and a tree
PREPARATION: Meditate to release the tension of the day

THE WORK:

1. Go to a tree and place the paper against its bark. Do a crayon or pencil rubbing of it.

2. Now sit with your back to the trunk, facing the sun, and place the image before you on the ground.

3. Relax your eyes and clear your mind. Patterns, images, or messages may appear.

4. Look to the sun as it goes down. The changing light may draw more from you. Look at the picture again and explore the design and everything it may say to you.

5. Once the sun has fully set, close your eyes and meditate on the picture, the sunset, and your connection to them. Once exhausted, bow to the tree and go on your way.

6. Repeat this process as often as you wish. It is most effective when done for at least 3 consecutive evenings.

Breaking Tension

(Willing yourself to solve problems and find peace in your ability to do so)

MATERIALS NEEDED: 3 sticks of varying sizes
PREPARATION: Take a nature walk and collect 3 sticks (1 thin one, 1 medium one, and 1 thicker one.) Best done during a waning moon cycle.

THE WORK:

1. Go before a comfortable tree and meditate on the sticks one at a time. Let the thin one represent the surface issues adversely affecting you— the little things. Let the middle one represent the deeper issues that are not life altering but still deeply problematic. Then let the thick one represent the worst of your troubles. It can be something from the past or recent times.

2. Lay them out in front of you. Place the thin stick to your left and the thick one on the right, with the mid-sized one appropriately in the middle.

3. Pick up the thin stick. Close your eyes and visualize your energies growing and overpowering the issue(s) represented in it. Simple solutions should come to mind. Let them guide you. Then open your eyes and break the stick. Chant, whisper, or sing of change and resolution.

4. Now, pick up the middle stick. Repeat the process as before but take more time to allow yourself to find the proper solution and truly envision it as a prophecy instead of just a mental image. Again, open your eyes and break the stick. Chant, whisper, or sing of change and resolution.

5. Last, pick up the thick stick. Again, do as before, closing your eyes to visualize the answers to this large infraction. It may take a lot of energy to fully realize the severity of the problem and even more so to come to a fully developed solution or series of methods for resolution.

6. When ready, open your eyes and break the stick. You may need to

stand up and balance the stick on the ground and step on it to sever the structure (depending on how thick it is).

7. Chant, whisper, or sing of freeing yourself from the burden you have carried under the weight of this great struggle.

8. Bow to the tree and carry out what must be done. This method can be performed as often as needed.

Flowering Finds to De-Stress in Spring

(For balance and appreciation of the simple things)

MATERIALS NEEDED: Find a flowering tree on public land or your own

PREPARATION: Meditate on the blooms of spring. To be done in the springtime.

THE WORK:

1. Stand before the tree and breathe in the fragrance of the flowers. Admire their fleeting beauty. Think of the work that goes into their creation and how they only paint the tree for a short time.

2. Now recall your recent stresses. Let them out. Push the electricity of anxiety, depression, and/or frustration up through your body and out with each exhale.

3. Focus on the issue that most discourages you and walk up to one of the flowers. Chant, sing, or whisper of the sacrifice of beauty and pluck the flower. Hold it in your palm and close your eyes. Brush your fingers

over the petals and let them absorb the stress from the situation.

4. Now close your hand over the flower, and hold it tight before letting it fall to the ground.

5. Repeat this process for the main problems surrounding your life, from the most detrimental to the least.

6. When finished, sit among the plucked flowers and thank them for their aid. Look to the tree and smile at its resilience and persistence. More flowers will grow. Better days will come. Balance is everywhere. Look around and feel that with all your senses.

7. Then gaze up beyond the tree. Bow and move on.

Capture and Release

(To release a bug outside when found inside for luck)

MATERIALS NEEDED: Cup and paper (optional)

PREPARATION: This situation is almost always random, so preparation is simply breathing deep and acknowledging the life and purpose that all creatures have.

THE WORK:

1. Whenever finding an insect or spider in the home or workplace, it's important to clear your mind.

2. Focus on the creature. Even if afraid of the specific type, extend your energies as you would to a friend or a trusted pet.

3. If knowledgeable and comfortable, gently hold out your hand and allow the bug to climb into your palm (this works best for crickets, ladybugs, and other harmless insects). Or gently place the cup over

the creature and slide the paper beneath to create a safe barrier. Then flip it and hold the paper over the top.

4. Walk to the nearest door, but speak to the insect as you do. Offer up kind words letting it know that you will set it free back in the outside world where it belongs.

5. Once outdoors, take it to a distant tree. Set it at the foot of the tree and bow to it. Chant, sing, or whisper of the power and security the tree will offer.

6. Take a moment to appreciate your role in life, then go about your business.

Tree Familiar

(To connect with a trusted tree and experience its wisdom)

MATERIALS NEEDED: A necklace or piece of jewelry and a tree that grows close to your home

PREPARATION: Best done during a waxing moon cycle. Set aside an ample span of time. Wear the piece of jewelry for at least a week.

THE WORK:

1. Go before the tree at dusk and face it with your back to the sun.

2. Sit directly in front of the trunk, holding the piece of jewelry in your hand.

3. Meditate on the object, then look at the tree. Talk to it like you would a trusted friend (as loud or quietly as desired). Start with simple details about your day and allow your energies to free themselves to

aid your tongue.

4. As you open up, lower your tone but continue sending out your energies until you are quiet and transmitting thought alone.

5. Stand and place a hand on the trunk. Gaze at the branches above you. Hang the piece of jewelry on one of the branches.

6. Close your eyes and think of the bauble as a gift or toy you would offer up to a trusted animal friend. Visualize it linking you physically.

7. Envision the electricity inside you flowing out with a great light. Seek out the tree's aura. Let them mingle.

8. Visit the tree every day. "Converse" with it as needed. Let it become a regular element of ritual and spellwork, but mainly your life.

Greening your Scene

(Bringing a potted tree into space for good fortune and quiet companionship)

MATERIALS NEEDED: Potted tree/plant

PREPARATION: Place the tree or plant in your workspace or home where it will be most useful.

THE WORK:

1. Every day, sit before the tree/plant and meditate on it. Clear your mind and allow the natural energies to connect.

2. Reach out and touch the branches or leaves. Stroke them gently.

3. Chant, whisper, or think up a rhyme that thanks the plant for offering positivity. Repeat these words until your head is light. Then close your eyes and center yourself.

4. Bow to the tree/plant and focus on the matters at hand.

Growing with Grace

(To draw from a tree's power and be more graceful)

MATERIALS NEEDED: Water and fruit (preferably picked yourself), a familiar tree

PREPARATION: Meditate on your present situation. What do you wish to keep, and what do you wish to change? Focus on these needs and wants in any area, career, family, friendships, etc.

THE WORK:

1. Go before a familiar tree. Place the water and the fruit at the roots.

2. Sit facing the tree, looking toward the sun.

3. Bless the water in the name of the Gods. Charge it with steady energies that flow and change as needed by pouring your power into it with the intention of facing the unknown.

4. Bless the fruit in the name of the elements. Charge it with growing powers that do not shift once fully developed by pushing your energies into it with the intention of repeating that you do not wish to change.

5. Stand and hold the water to the sky. Dip your fingers into the cup and sprinkle it on the ground beneath your feet. Chant, whisper, or sing of standing tall like the tree without constraints, reaching as far as you will.

6. Now drink the water until it is gone. Take as much time as needed. If compelled to sway or dance, follow the rhythm of magical intuition.

7. Kneel before the tree and hold up the fruit. Bite off a small piece and drop it onto the ground. Chant, whisper, or sing of rooting your values where they belong, so you do not grow too far from the spaces

that nourish you.

8. Feast upon the fruit until it is all devoured. Let each bite fill you with confidence in your future and remind you of where you came from.

9. When finished, sit before the tree and meditate on its example. Then bow to it and meet what is to come.

12

TREE MEANING
SPELLS

INDING MEANING IN MEDITATION AND RITUAL STRENGTHENS OUR spellwork. Spells are meant to sway the energies that encircle us and those we can help to aid in discovering/exploring truths that are just out of reach.

Opening myself to new purposes and responsibilities when walking with the trees becomes second nature. Their example is unchanging. They lean, bend, and even twist when required because it is what must be done. Those that do not fall when tested by the elements grow stronger. Spells that harness this power and transfer that breed of resilience into myself or those I work with speak directly to my spirit, my being. The air is right when casting a spell that is personally developed to suit specific needs like these ones do:

Channeling Strength

MATERIALS NEEDED: Blessed salt, blessed water, preferred cleansing herb, matches, a trusted dagger, a handful of dirt, and a trusted tree

PREPARATION: Bless the salt and water, and dig up dirt near the tree where this spell will be performed. Best done on a full moon or waxing cycle.

THE WORK:

1. Go before the tree as the sun goes down. Set up your materials on the ground at the foot of the tree, facing north with water to the west and salt to the east. Place the cleansing herb south and the dagger at the north, with the dirt in the center.

2. Stand before the grounded altar and welcome the Gods. Then cast a circle around the tree, sprinkling the salt, turning and sprinkling the water in the opposite direction.

3. Clear the air inside with the cleansing herb and sing, chant, or whisper of appreciating the elements' assistance. Dance around and ask for guidance in the journey of purpose and meaning for yourself or someone in need.

4. Now take up the dagger. Hold it to the sky and speak of the powers "as above," then bring it to the dirt at your feet and speak of the powers "and so below" to draw forth your energies.

5. Walk up to the trunk and press one hand to the bark. Connect your energies. Feel around for a weak spot of growth. This may take some time, but gently cut away that section of bark when found. (If one

cannot be found, cut a small twig from the nearest branch.)

6. Bring the cutting to your grounded altar and sit before it facing north. Place the dagger back in its spot and set the bark beside the dirt in the center.

7. Breathe deeply and meditate on the bark, and visualize its potential. Let it represent the possibilities. It can protect or rot. Grow solid or soft.

8. Now take up the dirt in both hands. Meditate on its neutral position. Focus your energies on discovering the best path for yourself or the one you are performing this spell for.

9. Slowly sprinkle it over the bark.

10. Holding it level, so as not to disturb the earth too much, bring the bark before you. Study how the soil has settled. Open your senses. Look for patterns and images. Blink with more than just the eyes you were given and feel the energies emanating from it. What is revealed?

11. Take as much time as needed but relax and close the circle once you become exhausted by taking up the dagger, touching its point to the ground and then above, thanking the Gods and slowly circling counterclockwise, speaking of "as above, and so below I close this sacred circle."

12. Ground yourself.

Finding Flexibility

(To become better equipped to handle life's changes/ struggles)

MATERIALS NEEDED: Blessed salt, blessed water, preferred cleansing herb, matches, a trusted dagger, a familiar tree, a piece of paper, and a garden shovel

PREPARATION: Bless the salt. Bless the water. Best done on a full moon or during the waxing cycle.

THE WORK:

1. Go before the tree at dawn. Set up your materials on the ground at the foot of the tree, facing south. Place the water to the west and the salt to the east. Place the cleansing herb south and the dagger at the north, with the paper in the center.

2. Stand before the grounded altar and welcome the Gods. Then cast a circle around the tree, sprinkling the salt, then turning and sprinkling the water in the opposite direction. Save a bit of each for further spellwork.

3. Clear the air inside with the preferred cleansing herb and sing, chant, or whisper of appreciating the elements' assistance. Stretch and center yourself to loosen the body and the mind.

4. Grasp the dagger and hold it to the sky, speaking of the powers "as above," then bring it to the dirt at your feet, speaking of the powers "and so below" to draw forth your energies.

5. Hold the dagger over the paper and press the tip into the center to puncture it. Then set it back in its place.

6. Walk within the circle looking for any fallen sticks or twigs. Choose only one and bring it before the paper at the grounded altar.

7. Kneel and meditate on the stick, its strength and growth. Now place the stick in the water. Pour the rest of the salt atop it. Chant, sing, or whisper a blessing for yourself or the person you are performing this spell for.

8. Now take up the stick and visualize it as the person needing to

find more flexibility. Hold it before the paper. Place one hand on the paper and charge it with the energy of change and strength through the ability to bend.

9. Carefully hold up the paper. (Fold it to fit the stick if needed.) Lay the stick along its top edge and roll it until completely covered with the paper. Hold this symbol up to the Gods. Ask for the intended outcome. Envision it for yourself or the one in need.

10. Grab a shovel and bury the paper-wrapped stick. As you dig, sing, chant, or whisper repeated rhyme about knowing when to bend and when to stand tall. New images and ideas will spark. They may come right away or be delayed, but they will come.

11. Once completely covered up, pat the soil and sit back. Break the circle and ground yourself.

Heeding the Calls Nearby

(To find direction and heighten intuition)

MATERIALS NEEDED: Single white candle, matches, leaf or pinecone (from a trusted tree), a cup of wine or water

PREPARATION: Meditate on the candle and infuse it with openness/your desire to connect with the Gods and do their/its bidding.

THE WORK:

1. Place the candle at the foot of a trusted tree. Set the wine in front of it and the leaf or pinecone between them in a simple line that leads to you.

2. Walk or around the tree three times chanting, singing, or whispering of your magical purpose.

3. Then kneel before the items and close your eyes. Meditate on the tree and what it means to you. Then extend your energies beyond earthly ties. Allow the same electricity that bonds you to bark and wood to the broader existence of the universe.

4. Speak to the powers of truth and eternity. Ask for clarity in your humbled state.

5. Gently take up the wine or water and pour a few drops on the leaf. Repeat a rhyme expressing the ties between life and all of creation. Examine how the liquid lands. Recognize any patterns or images presented.

6. Light the candle and meditate on this. Open your senses and listen for the answers that hide in everyday life.

7. Now pour a few drops over the candle, not trying to extinguish the flame, but if that occurs, so be it.

8. Call on the gods to expand your intuition. Ask them for stronger guidance. Then drink. Chant, sing, or whisper your devotion. Get up and dance, sway, or walk around the tree again, but in the opposite direction.

9. Bow to the tree, the universe, and yourself all at once.

Leaf Focus Spell

(For strengthening your attention span)

MATERIALS NEEDED: Blessed salt, blessed water, preferred

cleansing herb, matches, trusted dagger, familiar tree, a basket of leaves

PREPARATION: Best done during the fall or late summer. Bless the salt. Bless the water.

THE WORK:

1. Go to a familiar tree at dusk facing the sunset. Set the salt to the east, the water to the west, and the dagger north.
2. Cast a circle with salt, water, and your cleansing herb. Take up the dagger and ask the Gods to aid you "as above and so below," holding the blade up on "above" and down on "below.
3. Walk within the circle and collect as many leaves as possible, building your energies. Chant, sing, or whisper to the tree about your need to focus or help someone else regain their course.
4. Sit at the foot of the tree, looking out. Now gaze up to the network of branches and life overhead. Meditate on the patterns, grooves, and life surrounding you.
5. Let the electricity inside build and build.
6. Now dump the basket of leaves in your lap. Let them fall as they may. Focus on one. See it as yourself or the person in need. Fully connect your powers to the entire being.
7. Hold the leaf up and rock, repeating a rhyme of the importance of our path.
8. Now take up a second leaf. Visualize it as the first step toward the desired outcome. Lay it atop the first leaf (your person) and hold your hand over it, keeping the energies strictly honed on focus and determination.
9. Let the third leaf be the next step, and repeat the stacking process, but hold it in place, keeping the energies focused and honed on determination.
10. Repeat with as many leaves as needed.

11. When exhausted, scoop the pile of leaves into your hand. Stand and scatter them about you, dancing and laughing to send these energies into the world.

12. Bow to the tree. Thank it and the Gods. Close the circle and ground yourself.

Spell of Redemption

(To forgive yourself or others and allow for atonement)

MATERIALS NEEDED: A favored item/luck charm, a familiar tree, a basin of water, optional: paper of actions (if doing for someone else

PREPARATION: The person this is performed for must be truly ready for the full consequences of their actions and accept them with open senses and dignity. If performing for another, have them write out what they have done in great detail. Bless the water and set it at the tree's roots before beginning.

THE WORK:

1. Go before the tree and walk around it three times in one direction, then three times in the opposite. Once the energies are built, step closer to the tree inside the circled space.

2. Look to the trunk and bow your head. Close your eyes and recall how far you/the person involved has fallen.

3. Speak of each misdeed out loud. If doing this for another, read the details slowly.

4. Hold out the item/luck charm. Chant, sing, or whisper of offering the personal item as a sacrifice to what has been done.

5. Kneel before the basin of water Dip the offering in the purifying waters. Look at yourself in the ripples or envision the person in need in the ripples.

6. For the self: Now cup hands and dip them in the water. Spill the contents on each limb, then over the head chanting, singing, or whispering of a new start, of doing better. For others: fold up the paper and dip each corner into it, slowly visualizing the subject beginning anew. Then submerge the entire document for the person in need while chanting, singing, or whispering of redeeming the spirit that wishes to bathe in the realm of forgiveness.

7. Meditate on this new aspect. Hang the offering on the tree, then water the roots with the basin's contents.

8. Bow to the tree, thank the Gods and turn and walk with purpose.

Increasing Courage Spell

(For inner strength that can be expressed outwardly)

MATERIALS NEEDED: Blessed salt, trusted dagger, familiar tree
PREPARATION: Best done on a warm rainy summer day with no thunder and lightning, but it can also be done in the snow. Bless the salt.

THE WORK:

1. Take the salt and dagger to a trusted tree nearest to shelter in case the storm becomes electrical, and you need to move back inside.

2. Set the salt before you as you look to the tree. Hold the dagger out to it and chant, sing, or whisper of courage in all weather, no matter the cost. Stab the dagger into the ground to the handle sticks up.

3. Now take up the salt and walk around the dagger spilling salt in the name of the Gods and the power of the elements.

4. Face the tree and raise your arms while gazing into the grey sky above. Let the precipitation fall on your face. Visualize yourself standing firm no matter what comes. Pool your energies and let them fill you from limb to limb. Focus on elevating your energies to face anything head-on, no matter how your pulse races or your hands shake. Trust in the clouds and the passing of time that always guides truth and existence.

5. Walk up to the tree and place your hands, palms down, on the trunk. Repeat a rhyme to find courage strong like the base, steady like the trunk, and adventurous like the limbs.

6. Turn and walk around the dagger again in the opposite direction as before. Pull it from the ground. Hold it up to the sky and pledge to be brave no matter what.

7. Then return to shelter for a feast and grounding.

Spell to Draw Distant Friends, Family, Co-workers, or Neighbors Closer

(To be done when feeling distant and connections are fading)

MATERIALS NEEDED: Preferred cleansing herb, matches, a white candle, fresh picked/cut flowers, familiar tree

PREPARATION: Cut the flowers down to just the buds.

THE WORK:

1. Set a humble altar before your most trusted tree. Place the cleansing herb before it, then in a line, set the candles in front of the preferred cleansing herb, and last, the flower heads closest to you.

2. Light the cleansing herb and walk around the space chanting, singing, or whispering for the guidance of the Gods. Speak of cleansing the air for your magical purposes.

3. Return to your position in front of the line, closest to the flowers, and kneel before the tree. Gaze up at its majesty and center yourself.

4. Light the candle and meditate on it, focusing on the area of society you/the person in need wish(es) to better connect with. Visualize being with this group as you/they are. Envision becoming more rooted to these ties.

5. Now scoop the flower heads into your palms. Hold them close to you. Breathe in their fragrance. Close your eyes and let your energies grow. Feel the flowers' power, their symbolic meaning to life, death, and everything in between.

6. Now place each bud one by one in a circle around the candle. When set, get up and dance around the flowered candle, singing, chanting, or whispering about the love of others and the necessity for togetherness.

7. When at the peak of your movements, stop and hold your hands over the candle. Push all your caring energy into the purpose. Let it flow out of you and into the world for those you wish to be closer with or the individual seeking this outcome.

8. Sit and compose yourself. Open the circle and ground yourself.

Compassion Spell

(To increase empathy and focus on kindness)

MATERIALS NEEDED: Blessed salt, blessed water, preferred cleansing herb, matches, pulled weeds, trusted tree, honey, and milk

PREPARATION: Bless the salt. Bless the water. Pull up weeds from your garden or around your area while meditating on unearthing the reasons behind the frustration with another person/group. If performing for someone else, have them do the weeding and bring you the discarded plants.

THE WORK:

1. Set a humble altar at the foot of your favorite tree facing south. Set the water to the west, the salt to the east, the cleansing herb north, and the weeds directly in front of you to the south. Place the honey and milk in the center.

2. Cast a circle using the salt, water, and cleansing herb, asking the Gods to be with you and your work.

3. Kneel before the altar and gently press your hands to the weeds. Focus on the distance that builds between individuals when we allow our disagreements to overgrow.

4. Take up the weeds and soak them in the cup of milk. Meditate on nourishing resolution and more important connections.

5. Hold the honey and focus on its sweet healing power. Pour it over the soaking weeds. Chant, sing, or whisper of softening even the harshest feuds.

6. Pool your energies. Fix them on offering compassion for the person/

people in contention. Push this energy out through your fingertips into the mixture.

7. Now stand and take the mixture to the roots of the tree. Glance up at its great height. Ask it to protect your workings, and slowly pour the mixture around it.

8. Bow to the tree. Thank the Gods. Then close the circle and ground yourself.

Dislodging Mistrust

(To dispel paranoia)

MATERIALS NEEDED: Preferred cleansing herb, matches, mirror, veil or cloth to cover the mirror, familiar tree

PREPARATION: Meditate on the mirror to represent you or the person experiencing extreme mistrust.

THE WORK:

1. Place the mirror before the tree. Drape the veil, covering it.

2. Light the cleansing herb and walk around the trunk in a wide circle chanting, singing, or whispering for the elements to guide you and the Gods to bless your workings.

3. Now sit before the mirror. Hold your hands over it and visualize the distrust: the fear, misconceptions, or anger that feed it.

4. Build your energies, focusing on opening the self to overcome unfair blockades that have been placed between yourself/the person in need and others.

5. Grasp the veil covering. Chant, sing, or whisper of regaining the

trust needed to move forward with those who deserve it. Repeat these words as needed until you become lightheaded. Then close your eyes and remove the veil or covering.

6. Toss it aside.

7. Grip the mirror and hold it up to the trees. Stand and dance with it. Chant, sing, or whisper of unloading the burden of mistrust.

8. If doing for yourself: Hold the mirror to your face and truly see yourself from the inside out. If performing for another, caress the mirror and visualize the individual being freed from the inside out.

9. Then bow to the tree. Thank the elements and the universe for watching over you. Ground yourself and walk with ease.

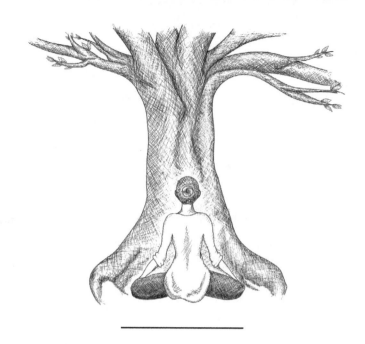

EXPANDING
PROGRESS WITH
TREES

THE MAGIC OF TREES LIVES WITHIN US BUT cannot flourish without proper nourishment. Our direct links to these life-supporting organisms vary based on location, upbringing, education, and many other factors. The industrial age pushed through innovations that forgot to leave space for many necessary forests. One of my favorite nature reserves was decimated by mining for building materials. The woodlands and entire ecosystem were blown up with sticks of dynamite, and destruction ruled in the name of "utilizing resources." It didn't take long for community leaders to realize their mistake. Over seventy-five years ago, a group of local businessmen took charge of the area. With the help of what is now known as the Missouri Department of Conservation, it was transformed into Rockwoods Reservation, a protected land that flourishes with life and wilderness as a successful restoration project: Missouri's first conservation area.

Like a trusted friend, I go to this area when in need. It reminds me that no matter what happens, growth and survival are possible under any circumstance. Walking the trails restores my faith. The dips and valleys remain, but the trees have reclaimed their space.

Places like this exist everywhere now. Parks and other lands left for the wild span in cities and states across the United States and beyond. They prove that humanity can build a world that heralds technology while respecting trees and the creatures they support.

Healing takes time, but there is always more to be done. To live at one with our natural side even while progressing into the future, greater initiatives are needed.

Currently, the U.S. government has tax breaks to incentivize building homes and industrial complexes with more energy efficiency. These programs have done wonders for expansion and reducing pollution, but we should preserve more areas to offer a cleaner and more balanced future.

Encouraging builders to plant trees around new developments in housing and business lots, as well as offering tax breaks or grants to those who leave at least one acre of land per subdivision/business complex, would limit deforestation, aid with protecting migratory patterns, improve air quality, and display enough greenery to aid mental health as well as physical health.

There are already programs committed to expanding tree planting across the globe. The 1 Trillion Tree initiative has been widely successful, planting over 35 billion new trees. If it continues, it will be a true gift to future generations, but we must keep the spirit of the movement alive.

There are meditations to help steady the mind and prepare the body and spirit for getting involved. Our intuition holds power to guide us far beyond what we know we are capable of. Tree Building Meditations are customized explicitly to step into the unknown and find and manage the best routes to discover, propose, and support causes that encourage incorporating tree planting into building plans.

Properly wording letters to officials and deciding the best phrasing to use when calling or meeting in person can be tricky. Campaigning for tax breaks and legislation to help with plant designs in new developments is work. Rituals to send out ideas for tree complexes have yet to be widely understood, but the correct energies will gain momentum and aid those who choose to push beyond.

Tree Building Spells come from the same electricity that originates from a lightning strike. The natural world is never forgotten where trees are concerned, but our focus must adapt and shift as quickly as the world around us. We can generate balance with the proper efforts.

13

TREE BUILDING MEDITATIONS

I T TAKES DETERMINATION, LEADERSHIP, AND POISE TO GAIN SUPPORT FROM others. When working to find solutions and present them in a palatable manner, a proper plan isn't all a person needs. A relatable dialogue with realistic goals and balance defines success rates. Balance is the main factor.

In faith and spirituality, one can lose their footing. That's why grounding is so important. Our relationship with the trees reminds us to aim high while remaining rooted in what nurtures us. Meditation allows me to walk with the gods and continue my journey through the tangible world. I can fly free without ever moving from a comfortable space. Grasping at ideas and discovering the steps needed to make a vision reality are all alive in this spark of the spirit. These meditations embody that:

Seeking Solutions

(To find greater purpose in problem-solving)

Step 1: Visit a nearby park and find a quiet spot to sit or stand with the trees.

Step 2: Breathe deep and let your energies build. Reach out to the nearest tree and close your eyes. Imagine the power within flowing out in a brilliant light and wrapping around the tree.

Step 3: Push that power up and out through the canopy to seek a broader network of connections. Feel the consistency of the Gods.

Step 4: Chant, sing, or whisper words asking for specific ideas that aid the cause of forestry. Allow yourself to walk through the possibilities. Concentrate on visualizing your individual role as well as the greater scale.

Step 5: When exhausted, open your eyes and look above. Study the patterns of the leaves and branches above. Let them whisper to you.

Step 6: Slowly draw yourself back. Place your palms on the ground and focus on the physical elements surrounding you. Then move on.

Strengthening Your Role

(To strengthen your greater purpose and encourage community involvement)

Step 1: Early in the morning, when you wake, sit at the foot of the bed. Straighten your spine. Root your feet to the floor, let your hair branch out as you close your eyes, and allow the passage from sleep to consciousness to aid in this meditation.

Step 2: Close your eyes and feel the light of day. Let it wash over you, enter your mind.

Step 3: Clear away the confusion or dreams of the night before. Focus on what truly matters to you and how your role in the world matters in the great work of existence.

Step 4: Visualize the ideas or plans you have entertained concerning connecting to nature and advancing its role in society. Take the solutions from the previous mediation and expand on them. Let the future unfold within your mind.

Step 5: Now, bow your head. It may be helpful to rock back and forth to build energy. Draw out your truth. Can you commit to this? Are you wholly capable of taking on this task?

Step 6: The answer may not be desirable. In situations where the vision is too much, allow reality to comfort you. If fully available, sing, whisper, or declare your dedication mentally or physically.

Step 7: Relax and open your eyes. Stretch and smile on the new day.

Finding Reality in Your Vision

(To gain confidence in your goals and make a solid plan to carry them out)

Step 1: Stand before the nearest window to your sleeping space before bed. If possible, gaze out to a tree or multiple trees. Study how their shadows represent them.

Step 2: Close your eyes. Envision your shadow as a symbol of what has been and may come.

Step 3: Focus on how you have grown. Allow the inner calling to draw forth the electricity from inside. What has sparked success? What failures have dimmed?.

Step 4: Allow your connection to the tree(s) to guide you toward finding realistic options for new plans to aid them. Allow past mistakes to remain present in thought as guides for avoiding the same blunders.

Step 5: As things become clearer, voice them to yourself. Speak of step-by-step options.

Step 6: When fully defined, breathe deep, and open your senses. Write down this plan and leave it by your bedside for the night to clarify.

Bolstering Plans

(To build confidence and follow through)

Step 1: Take your written/typed plans before a familiar tree. Sit comfortably beneath the boughs.

Step 2: Study each point and relax your eyes. Read each step aloud, repeating the plans again and again like an incantation until your eyes relax and you find yourself in a trance-like state.

Step 3: Close your eyes and see yourself making this idea a reality. Tangibly.

Step 4: Extend your energies beyond yourself and to the tree. Open your senses to hear the tree's voice connect with its energies. Let it comfort and support you.

Step 5: Tell yourself to follow the steps. Repeat them again. Tell yourself to find success. Repeat the steps again. Tell yourself to support your inner workings. Repeat the steps again.

Step 6: Now lie back and gaze up at the greenery, ready to act.

Connecting to the Forest of Humanity

(Preparing for social work)

Step 1: Sit beneath a tree near your home, back to the trunk facing out. Breathe deep and focus your energies on seeking others.

Step 2: Gaze to any sidewalks, roads, or neighboring homes, thinking of how trees reach for each other as they grow higher and higher (if in a rural area, visualize them). Humans often find more success when working together as well. Meditate on this energy and work to send it out into the space around you and beyond.

Step 3: Close your eyes and let the inner light guide you toward whom to seek and how to find them. Neighbors, businesses, and local officials should become clearer in your mind.

Step 4: Open your eyes and relax. Wave if others pass you. Offer a friendly aspect.

Step 5: Stand and be ready to take the first step toward building deeper connections with the forest of humanity that spans before you.

.

Taking Action

(Reflecting on progress)

Step 1: Once you begin speaking with those willing to consider your ideas take a walk in a community park or forest.

Step 2: With each breath, meditate on these actions and how they further the course of what needs to be done.

Step 3: Visualize gaining momentum and further support. See the product of your vision as you walk. Let it engulf you between reality and what will be.

Step 4: If encountering any animals or obstructions on this walk, stop and appreciate the experience. Fallen logs sometimes host special purposes. Deer are the friends of healers. Squirrels bound before innovators. Take notice of these energetic familiars and the power they add to your goal.

Fertilizing Your Efforts

(To build mental strength and heighten intuition)

Step 1: Stand before a familiar tree. Breathe deep and pool your energies. Let the wooden giant renew your strength.

Step 2: Open your senses and step closer to the tree. Touch it with one hand and hold the other out. Allow yourself to be a conductor sending and receiving messages.

Step 3: Push out the hopes you hold for your project. Pour it into the tree and the air.

Step 4: Now close your eyes and focus on listening with all aspects of your being. Hear the trees and the atmosphere's messages. Be communicative of all possible outcomes to prepare yourself for what is ahead.

Step 5: Sit and rub your hands on the ground. Relax. Enjoy the calm surrounding you. Accept that no matter what happens, your efforts matter.

Meditate from Seed to Tree to Celebrate Success

(To accept your success and be happy)

Step 1: Find a seed pod, pinecone, or nut that has dropped from a tree. Take it home and set it before you.

Step 2: Hold your hand over it and feel its energy. Connect your power to it. Allow your senses to open and mingle, focusing on recent successes and the blooming of your idea.

Step 3: Pool all your electricity together. Visualize it as a glowing light and push it into the seed.

Step 4: Feel the vibrations grow around you. Hold the seed in your palms and bring it to your chest to strengthen the bond. Let it represent the meaning of your ability to make your thoughts a reality.

Step 5: When exhausted, place the seed in a spot of importance: on an altar, desk, mantle, etc. Leave it as a symbol of possibilities and your role in experiencing them.

Renewing Roots to Overcome Failure

(To overcome project failures/compromise to make

Step 1: Go before a familiar tree. Bow to it and kneel at its roots. Place your hands on them and close your eyes.

Step 2: Open your senses and call to the tree's energies. Ask it for aid and direction.

Step 3: Feel the vibrations of life before you. Let them envelop you.

Step 4: Ask the Gods to offer insight. Seek understanding from the root of your cause and why it did not produce a tall firm outcome.

Step 5: Meditate on the failures of points that did not lead to compromise and advancement. Let the tree's power and direct link to the universe guide you toward wise conclusions and hope for other attempts.

Step 6: Open your eyes and relax. Feel the earth beneath you and smile at the sky above.

14

TREE COMPLEX
RITUALS

ONORING AND ENCOURAGING GREEN SPACES IN A COMMU-
NITY or area holds a special purpose. The more energy we
put into our connection with nature and the elements,
the better we understand our specific needs and path.
The trees that surround my home are trusted friends. I also have plans
to plant more, and as my own space develops into a garden of beauty
and love, my neighbors recognize the positive energy and follow suit.

When I lived in an apartment complex, suggestions to plant more
trees or host a community garden received mixed reviews. Rituals to
support these ideas, aid them in coming to fruition and honor what is
growing offer support from the powers that be when other people are
less than eager. They can also give individuals the insight they need to
know when and what to pursue.

Planting the Vision

(To brainstorm and focus on goals)

MATERIALS NEEDED: Tree, black ribbon, and wine or water
PREPARATION: Perform during a new moon or early waxing moon when the sky is dark.

THE WORK:

1. Stand before the tree and hold up the drink. Ask the Gods to be with you.

2. Now walk around the tree three times in one direction, then three times in the other. As you do this, chant, sing, or whisper repeated phrases encouraging tree-planting ideas to grow from the seeds of your being.

3. Now kneel before the tree. Place the drink to your left and hold up the ribbon. Meditate on it as a link to the sky. Let it represent the unknown and the future that will come to be no matter what.

4. Tie the black ribbon around your wrist and drink the wine or water. Sip it slowly, contemplating the tree before you. Allow your connection to grow and reveal what is necessary.

5. Feel your energies extending. Let them glow. Continue this search until exhausted. Do not be upset if the mind wanders. Concise thoughts may present themselves in dreams once you go to sleep.

6. When finished, stand and bow to the tree.

Gaining Support

(To build confidence and reach out to others)

MATERIALS NEEDED: Journal or notebook, Garden shovel, Cup of milk

PREPARATION: Perform on the waxing moon.

THE WORK:

1. Sit before the tree and meditate on your purpose.

2. Take up the journal and write a list of people who will support you on one side of a piece of paper, then on the back, write a list of people you need to contact to bolster support. Ex: Community leaders, city representatives, etc.

3. Fold the paper in half twice, then press between palms. Build your energies until they flow through you like a glowing light. Now push that power into the paper, focusing on the people individually and then as a whole group.

4. Dig a hole before the tree. Look up to it and chant, sing, or whisper your intentions. Ask for it to spread the message through its vast network of roots.

5. Place the list in the hole, then take a sip of the milk. Let the nourishment sink into you. Now pour the rest over the paper and repeat an incantation to gain support.

6. Fill in the hole and place your hands on top of it. Visualize others coming to aid the call.

7. Bow to the tree and walk on.

Growing Understanding Sigil

(To better connect with the gods and your purpose)

MATERIALS NEEDED: Pen, paper, sigil, clippings from your garden or plant, a familiar tree

PREPARATION: Create a sigil to represent the expansion of your project. Perform during the waxing moon period at dawn.

THE WORK:

1. Walk around a trusted tree and greet it. Breathe deep and look to the sky. Welcome the Gods.

2. Kneel before the tree and place the clippings before you. Take your pen and paper and draw your sigil as small as possible.

3. Meditate on the image, the idea. Think of the basis. It's simplest meaning.

4. Now draw the sigil again, but this time larger. Meditate on this larger image and focus on making it a reality. Think of the connection to others. How it can develop deeper ties.

5. Once more, draw the sigil but make it as large as possible. Meditate on the enormity of the need. Think of it becoming a reality through great effort. See yourself growing and changing along with the task.

6. Lay the images before you and take up the garden clippings. Draw energy from the plants.

7. Now gently drop them in the middle of the images. Sing, chant, or whisper of expanding with the aid of the elements.

8. Fold the corners of the paper in, wrapping the clippings up. Fold it in half and place the paper on your altar or in a place of importance in your home. It may be burned at the next full moon fire.

Renewing Strength

(To be done during a full or waxing moon to build courage)

MATERIALS NEEDED: Tree, tall stick/branch that measures up to your shoulder and is suitable to serve as a staff

PREPARATION: Do on the full moon or during the waxing cycle at night.

THE WORK:

1. Stand before the tree facing the moon. Hold the stick up to the sky and chant, sing, or repeat incantation of standing tall no matter what winds blow to knock you down.

2. Walk or dance around the tree with the stick at your right side, moving to the right, building up energy, and going around as many times as desired. All the while connecting your energies to the tree.

3. Now turn and do the same, moving left AND holding the stick out to your left. Expel any doubts that may weigh down your cause.

4. Walk closer to the tree trunk. Hold one end of the stick and press the other to the tree trunk. Close your eyes and call upon the elements. Ask the Gods to solidify your purpose and grant proper resolve.

5. Bow to the tree and step back. Kneel with the stick standing up. Let it serve as a reminder of your strength when you feel weak.

Drawing Compromise

(For balancing energies to make reasonable compromises)

MATERIALS NEEDED: String, 2 small twigs of the same size
PREPARATION: Best to be done on a new moon or during the waning phase.

THE WORK:

1. Stand before a familiar tree. Call upon the corners of the elements and ask the tree to shelter you.

2. Place the materials at your feet and raise your arms to the sky. Chant, sing, or repeat incantation of balance and compromise. Let the words flow freely and organically.

3. Then kneel on the ground. Drape the string over your lap and hold one stick in each hand. Let one stick represent your vision, and the other stick represent the obstacles before it. Focus all your power on finding the middle ground on your issue so it can become a reality. Pour that great electricity into the sticks.

4. Now take up the string and tie a stick on each end.

5. Hold the center of the string until each end is as equal as can be. Look to the sky and chant for balance in your being, mission, and outcome.

6. Watch the twigs dance before you as they dangle. Take in their connection to the tree and the greater work.

7. Hang the sticks on a low branch, keeping each side as equal as possible. Then walk, skip, or dance around the tree, releasing any pent-up energy.

8. When exhausted, bow to the tree, turn to the sticks and nod at their purpose.

Start to Finish Ritual

(Ritual to solidify a project so it will be carried out properly)

MATERIALS NEEDED: Dagger, trusted tree, honey
PREPARATION: Perform on the new moon or waxing phase at nighttime. Charge the honey with solidifying energy.

THE WORK:
1. Set the honey at the food of the tree. Hold the dagger up and declare your work "as above," then stab the dagger into the earth before you as you declare your purpose "as below."
2. Ask the tree to deliver the power of the elements with the aid of the gods.
3. Then kneel and meditate on seeing your cause carried out and finalized.
4. Take up the dagger and draw a symbol of your work being fulfilled in the dirt with the point. Gently bring the point close and let it rest over your heart. Chant, sing, or whisper of your passion for this purpose.
5. Then put the point back into the dirt and draw a circle around the symbol. Trace the circle as many times as needed, again and again pouring your energies into the soil for a better outcome.
6. When ready, set the dagger to your left and take up the honey. Cover the circle and the symbol drawn inside with honey while chanting an

incantation of sealing what is to be.

7. Sit back and ground yourself.

Honoring Success

(To give thanks for success)

MATERIALS NEEDED: Water or wine, a picture or item from a successful site (like a rock, etc.), a familiar tree near your home, small feast

PREPARATION: Perform on a full moon or waxing cycle. Prepare the feast and set it up outside or indoors.

THE WORK:

1. Go before the tree and stand facing the moon. Place the drink to your left and the item/picture to your right.

2. Walk around the tree, slowly taking in the accomplishment. Then turn and walk back in the opposite direction.

3. Kneel and take up the item or picture, chant, speak, or whisper thanks to the Gods and the elements that brought this success. Celebrate this victory through dance and/or meditation.

4. Then take up the wine/water and toast the future. Now go and feast with thoughts of good health.

Finding a Better Way when Things Fall Through

(A release from negative outcomes)

MATERIALS NEEDED: Trusted tree, nuts, and berries

PREPARATION: Mix the nuts and berries. Meditate on them and charge with energy to carry on. Perform on a new or waning moon cycle.

THE WORK:

1. Take the mix before the tree. Walk up to the trunk and press one palm against the trunk. Chant, whisper, or sing of your failure.

2. Step back and ask the Gods to bless a better way.

3. If doing this as a group, have each person stand with their back to the tree and walk to the four corners in this fashion, or it may be done in solitary: Turn away from the tree and slowly walk toward the north. With each step, call upon the element of earth, dropping nuts and berries as an offering. Then walk back to the tree.

4. Walk toward the east. With each step, call upon the power of air and drop a portion of the nuts and berries to solidify your rite. Return to the tree.

5. Walk back to the tree, then turn toward the south. With each step, call upon the element of fire and drop your offering. Return to the tree once more.

6. Lastly, turn to the west and call upon the power of water as you drop your nuts and berries. Then come back to the tree trunk.

7. Face the tree once more and raise your arms to the sky. Pool your energies until they vibrate within. Now reach down to the ground and

send out that electricity. Let it go into the earth and spread beneath you.

8. Bow to the tree. Thank the Gods and ground yourself.

Blessing What is Built

(To be done at dawn to bless the fruits of your labors)

MATERIALS NEEDED: Water, salt, pine or rose oil

PREPARATION: Preparation: Perform at first light. This can be as elaborate or discreet as you wish.

THE WORK:

1. Greet the building/complex/area. Smile and meditate on its energies.

2. Take up the water and pour a small amount into your hands. Toss up and down. Whisper, chant, or sing of blessing what has come to be.

3. Take up the salt and pour a small handful into your palm. Toss it to your right, then your left, meditating on the energies that brought this new development into existence.

4. Now walk around the space. Let a drop of oil fall every few feet and whisper, chant, or sing of blessing the past, present, and future with the honor of the trees.

15

TREE COMPLEX SPELLS

ROM START TO FINISH, GETTING BACKING FOR A tree planting project takes time. Urban areas often require more plan-
ning because there are extra factors to consider. Encouraging
builders and government officials to support these kinds of
endeavors is a challenging task. It takes a true will.

To solidify a commitment to your ideas, meditation and ritual build
stronger bonds, but spellwork is a direct link between them and future
realities. Focus and divinity lead toward fully developed connections.
Casting spells to plot, push, and perform acts that bring trees into
society's building plans sets nature and technology in harmony. They
are not always necessary but helpful tools when meeting unyielding
obstacles.

Protecting Progress Spelll

(To balance new outcomes and protect them as they shape the future)

MATERIALS NEEDED: Salt, water, preferred cleansing herb, dagger, leaves and or sticks and twigs from a trusted tree, 1 black candle and 1 white candle, matches, garden shovel

PREPARATION: Bless the salt and water. Set your altar with the black and white candles at the head facing north, the salt to the east, water to the west, the dagger at the south, and the preferred cleansing herb in the center with the tree items scattered around it.

THE WORK:

1. Cast a circle with the salt and water. Cleanse the area with the preferred cleansing herb and call the corners. Chant, sing, or whisper for the Gods to protect your magical workings.

2. Take the dagger and hold it up. Invoke the right of "as above," then hold it to the ground and invoke the right of "and so below," now tap the edge of the blade to the leaves, sticks, and/or twigs, slowly connecting your energies to each.

3. Set the blade down and light the candles calling for balance to protect the progress you wish to make through your endeavor.

4. Meditate on the candles and mingle your energies. Let your power flow freely, and explore whatever comes to mind.

5. When ready, gather the tree items in a clump at the center of the altar. Grasp the black candle and repeat an incantation of sealing protection for your project. Pour wax over the items to bind them together as you visualize your cause to plant more trees.

6. Breathe deep. Steady yourself. Now grasp the white candle and do the same with it.

7. Let the wax melt and relax. Open the circle and ground yourself. Let the candles burn down.

8. The next day, when completely extinguished, use the dagger to break the wax from the surface and keep the tree items sealed together. Bury beneath a friendly tree.

Spell to Find the Right Design/Hook

(To aid with marketing and gaining support for a new idea)

MATERIALS NEEDED: Salt, water, pen, paper/notebook, leaves and or/or sticks and twigs from a trusted tree, luck rock (rock with a hole through it), 4 green altar candles

PREPARATION: Bless the salt and water. Place the altar candles at the four corners. Set the salt at the east area of the center, the water to the west area of the center, place the rock at the northern area of the center, and the tree items closer to the couth area. Keep all items safely pushed further in than the candles. The pen and paper should lay before the altar.

THE WORK:

1. Cast a circle with the salt and water. Call the corners and ask the Gods to be with you during your workings.

2. Then stand with the pen holding it up like a dagger. Chant, sing, or

whisper for the proper inspiration to reach success.

3. Bend down and hold the pen over the paper. Chant, sing, or whisper of the great connection you wish to perceive.

4. Place the pen on the paper. Go around and light the candles. Let their energy touch you and inspire you. Dance or move around the circle if compelled to do so.

5. When ready, sit with the pen and paper and meditate on the tree items. Once properly focused, take up the luck rock and look at the altar through the hole in the solid mass. Relax your eyes and study the leaves and/or sticks and twigs. Really see them and their purpose.

6. As ideas come, write them down. This is a spell to aid with wording, so don't be afraid to write as much as possible. The point is to let the voice of the cause come through in terms that best reach the widest audience possible.

7. When exhausted, set the pan and paper down. Breathe deep and open the circle. Ground yourself, then blow out the candles.

Spell to Search for Support

(For developing new connections with community members)

MATERIALS NEEDED: Salt, water, preferred cleansing herb, matches, 9 ribbons or pieces of sting of all colors, including black and white, trusted tree

PREPARATION: Bless the salt and water. Do it on a clear night under a waxing or full moon.

THE WORK:

1. Go before the tree and set up a mini altar at its roots. Place the salt to the east, the water to the west, the ribbons to the south, and face the tree placing it at the northern head. Set the preferred cleansing herb and matches in the center of the materials.

2. Now cast a circle using the salt and water. Calling upon the Goddess to be with you in the name of the elements. Then light the preferred cleansing herb and cleanse the space. Dance and twirl with the smoke to build energy.

3. Put the preferred cleansing herb out and kneel before the ribbons/string. Lay each across your lap and take one up at a time. Meditate on the ribbon/string as a different group of people. Let each color represent the personalities you wish to draw closer within your community. Visualize developing new connections and send out that energy.

4. When each ribbon/string is finished, stand with them and hang them on the tree limbs. Chant, sing, or whisper for the courage and ability to reach out and draw people who will lend their support to you.

5. Once all are tied, take a step back and focus on the tree's beauty. Study how the moonlight affects the colors tied to the tree.

6. Bow to your need and thank the tree for standing tall. Raise your arms to the sky and open the circle.

7. Gaze at the vastness above and breathe deep. Ground yourself and prepare to take the initiative in meeting new people throughout the near future.

Leadership Incantation

(For confidence and unity)

MATERIALS NEEDED: A drum of any kind, homemade or store-bought, pen and paper, and a friendly tree.

PREPARATION: PPerform on a sunny day under a preferred tree. Invite as many people as you wish or none.

THE WORK:

1. Sit before the tree. Rub the top of your drum and breathe deep.

2. Now slap out a simple beat. Let it start slow and rhythmic. Entrance yourself/selves.

3. Add more elaborate hits and speed the process until in perfect synchronicity. Focus on leading your own band. Realize the importance of balance and its role in aiding influential people.

4. Sing, chant, or whisper the words that come. Let the wrap around you and the music. Fall in love with each sound and customize the lyrics to grow your strength in directing others.

5. Take the song as far as it will go. When exhausted, rest and write down the words that accompanied your hands.

6. Repeat for as long as needed. Remember to write the lyrics for each session out individually.

7. Keep these close. You may need to read them when doubts seep through.

Reaching Further Spell

(To find the courage to speak with leaders to create positive change))

MATERIALS NEEDED: Water, salt, preferred cleansing herb, a single brown candle, matches, garden shovel, list of officials you wish to contact (make sure it's a duplicate, not your only copy), and a trusted tree

PREPARATION: PBless the water and salt. Carve a tree on the sides of the brown candle to represent the project you wish to get support for. Set your altar with the brown candle at the center. Place the water to the west, the salt to the east, the list to the north with the garden shovel on top, and the preferred cleansing herb and matches at the south.

THE WORK:

1. Cast a circle with salt and water, asking the gods to bless your purpose.

2. Call the corners and light the cleansing herb. Cleanse the space with the aid of the elements.

3. Grab the garden shovel and hold it up like a dagger. Touch its point to the paper and chant, sing, or whisper of the connections that are made above and below.

4. Now light the brown candle in honor of the trees that inspire your work. Kneel before it and meditate on strengthening your reach. Visualize yourself successfully speaking with leaders and local officials to make positive changes that benefit greenery.

5. Now take up the list and hold it before the light. Read the names

like an incantation. Repeat them with vigor and declare the will to reach them.

6. Open the circle and let the candle burn down as you go to bury the list at the foot of a familiar tree.

Swaying Skeptics

(A spell to help others see your point of view)

MATERIALS NEEDED: Water, salt, Flowers (preferably hand-picked), trusted tree

PREPARATION: Bless the salt and water. Set the flowers at the foot of the tree.

THE WORK:

1. Cast a circle with the salt and water. Call upon the Gods to offer strength through the powers of the elements.

2. Pick up each flour one by one. Let every individual stalk represent one of the people who oppose you or any doubts you continue harboring against yourself.

3. Sit and meditate on the root of this opposition/negativity. Visualize the cure to these issues.

4. Hold the flowers up to the sky and breathe deeply. Chant, sing, or whisper the power of truth. Let it grow within you. Build up your energies and push that electricity from your core through your fingertips, through the stalks, into the blossoms, and beyond.

5. Look to the tree and see how its great height shelters the flowers and trust in its bounty. Stand and dance with the flowers in the circle. Let

them bow and sway. See yourself applying this rhythm to your cause and winning over skeptics.

6. Lay the flowers in a ring around the tree trunk. Bow to the tree and place your palms at its roots. Release all your energies into the roots and the world beyond.

7. Open the circle and ground yourself.

Spell to Utilize Failure as Fuel

(For finding a new approach when an endeavor fails)

MATERIALS NEEDED: Water, salt, a handful of dirt, a stick from a friendly tree, a bowl, a beeswax candle, matches, and a garden shovel

PREPARATION: Bless the salt and water. Set the altar with the dirt in the bowl and the stick at the north, water to the west, candle to the south, and salt to the east. Best done on a new or waning moon.

THE WORK:

1. Cast a circle with the salt and water. Call the corners and ask for the gods' guidance.

2. Now light the candle and chant an incantation of accepting your failure for a project that has fallen through. Let the light warm you and inspire you beyond the end of this attempt.

3. Take up the bowl of dirt and sit. Place your fingertips atop the soil and feel the neutralizing energy. Let your own power balance within. Set the bowl down.

4. Now grasp the stick. Let it remind you of what it was once a part of

and that breaking does not end its purpose. It just changes it. Stand and walk, sway, or dance around the altar.

5. When the circle is filled with electricity, stop and touch the stick to the dirt. Break the stick and take up the handful of earth. Set the stick's pieces at the bottom of the bowl and drop the dirt over them.

6. Take the candle and pour wax over the dirt-covered sticks. Chant, sing, or whisper of fertilizing related ideas that may host more power.

7. Open the circle and leave the candle to burn out. Take the bowl to the tree and bury its contents at the roots, concentrating on new sparks that may fly from this sealed flame.

Success for all Seasons Spell

(To increase your ability to succeed)

MATERIALS NEEDED: Water, salt, preferred cleansing herb, matches, small cup or plate of ice, flowers (hand-picked preferred), a yellow candle, leaves from a trusted tree

PREPARATION: Bless the salt and water. Set the altar with the water to the west, the salt to the east, the preferred cleansing herb to the north, and matches at the south, then arrange/decorate the center with the symbols of the season. Perform on a full moon or waxing moon cycle.

THE WORK:

1. Cast a circle with the salt and water. Call the corners and invite the Gods to offer their blessings.

2. Light the preferred cleansing herb and cleanse the altar with it.

3. Hold up the ice and chant, sing, or whisper of the power of the winters to come.

4. Hold up the flowers and chant, sing, or whisper of the energy spring brings.

5. Light the candle and kneel before it. Focus on the light and chant, sing, or whisper of the electricity connecting everything to the sun and all of existence.

6. Now take up the leaves. Step back from the altar to avoid the flames and toss them into the air above you, chanting, singing, or whispering of the spirit of autumn eternal.

7. Dance, sway, or move about as compelled to do so. Let your spirit free. Then stop and push that great power toward the altar reciting an incantation of your project's success and the impact it will have.

8. When exhausted, open the circle and ground yourself.

Sealing the Future

(To protect your impact for generations to come)

MATERIALS NEEDED: Jar of dirt/grasses from the site where the development/tree project is constructed, lavender flowers, water, salt, quartz rock/crystal

PREPARATION: Perform beneath a trusted tree. Bless the water and salt. Perform on a full moon.

THE WORK:

1. Go to the tree and place the jar at the foot. Set the lavender in front of the jar and the quartz in front of the plant in a line.

2. Take up the salt and carefully dump it into the water. Then walk

around the tree three times, sprinkling slight drops around.

3. Ask the universe to hear your call. Then kneel before the line of items.

4. Meditate on the quartz and its protective powers. Offer it your trust. Then place it in the jar and ask it to watch over the site where the contents originated from.

5. Now take up the lavender. Feel its protective energy. Share your own with it. Mingle the power until your body is warm with safety and love. Then place it in the jar and ask it to preserve the site where the dirt/grasses originally resided.

6. Close up the jar. Then take the last of the salt water and pour it over the sealed top as you offer up every bit of strength you have to the thought of protecting the space you helped create for future generations.

7. Meditate on the jar and its meaning. When exhausted, sit back and ground yourself.

8. Set/bury/or sink the jar in a safe place.

ROOTING PREGNANCY POWERS WITH TREE ENERGY

ALL MATTER IS CONNECTED. WHETHER LIVING OR NOT, each mass hosts energy and/or influences the beings around it. That energy determines many factors. Power, ability, interaction, and purpose all spark from the energy within and the energy surrounding a creature.

Having covered the planet for centuries, trees host incalculable power. The oldest living roots on the planet date back to ancient Egypt.

If age comes with wisdom, humanity will benefit from paying more attention to their branchy neighbors. Every major religion has text about trees or a special tree. Every culture has records of the significance of trees.

Recognizing the sheer electricity held within a sprout or great trunk draws forth instincts and natural ability. Grooves along the grains are like their own language. They support numerous creatures and countless lives without the need for a brain, complex communication, or verbal language.

They may seem primitive, but trees represent the entirety of wholeness. They host their own network. It has recently been theorized that these great giants look out for one another, even without neurons. They move aside to allow other trees sunlight and weave roots together to connect their nutrients and lives, but the most fascinating power of all is their use of fungus as an "internet."

Releasing certain chemicals and hormones, trees can shoot out electrical signals to one another. When a tree that has spanned its life connected to another dies, the other follows shortly after. There have even been cases of surrounding trees working together to produce the proper environment for certain mosses and lichens to grow over stumps like a grave marker, as if a sign of mourning.

These interactions are more than just physical; they are emotional. There is a consciousness that pulses beside the man-made world completely undetected.

The knowledge and communal life harbored within the forests presents an example for all who wish to learn. It is pure magic. The idea that plants, which have no thought process in terms of the human brain, feel their way through life in a way that proposes emotion and consciousness upsets everything the scientific world believes about existence. It leads one to question their purpose.

I remember when I found myself wondering, "If a creature can host so many similar qualities to humans even with a very different biological structure, wouldn't that mean that people themselves contain a spiritual aspect that goes beyond physical limitations?"

Trees are more than just oxygen givers. That remarkable feat provides life to numerous creatures, but they interconnect the underground world. They know the sky. And for those who reach beyond the barriers set before them by modernity, a secret language can be felt and absorbed.

Too often, the human world obsesses with the surface. We concern ourselves with what is right in front of us and miss out on a vast world of sensations.

From the moment we root ourselves into our mother's womb, other abilities sprout and hold the potential for a greater understanding. We stretch our limbs and begin our journey into the world.

At birth, we are more apt to absorb everything presented to us. Our brain contains about as many neurons as it will ever have. That's roughly 100 billion neurons. Everything a child experiences shapes how they see the world, but like our tree friends, no matter what trauma and trials we suffer as we develop, there is room for healing, regrowth, and natural magic.

Most children find it easier to talk to animals and plants. Adults are often busy or condescending and sometimes laugh at immature whimsy, but exploration requires suspending disbelief and opening themselves up to new ideas and experiments.

The teenage years are wrought with confusion and frustration. Nearing adulthood while still not fully developed is a tough task for anyone. Solitude and escaping ridicule or self-doubt is a necessity. If, instead of pulling away from the resources that have aided adolescents for generations, families and friends rededicated themselves to the energies gifted by the trees, this period of life becomes less tumultuous because it offers a stronger sense of self. It reminds one of their purpose and all the power they may harness.

Whether one finds their way back to the rites of tree adoration in childhood, during maturity, or adulthood, the messages exchanged between the perceptive tree lover and the woods are absolute truths. How one interacts with the rooted giants determines what they discover.

Some spend their entire lives oblivious to the great knowledge flowing through the universe. It is always a choice. No matter how buried, human instinct calls to it.

Once a person allows themselves to at least consider what exists beyond sight, interactions shift, purposes grow more defined, powers reveal, abilities refine, and the true ritual of existence begins. Trees feel the electricity in the air. They absorb and utilize it. Humans are also energy conductors and can harness that source through their daily interactions, but it takes time, effort, and respect for the entire universe.

How we interact with our surroundings, and trees primarily, determines what kind of life they will lead. Many people pass by trees every day without really seeing them. There is a difference between walking, driving, or going by something, minutely letting the image pass, and stopping to touch, acknowledge, and speak with it. Those who carve out time to talk to the trees and reach out to the natural world gain heightened intuition. Our instincts are called to the surface. Reason and understanding present themselves through the calm, gentle nature of the earth organically.

These interactions are not to be taken for granted. They remind an individual to breathe deep and truly live. Consciously connecting with trees pulls forth one's spirit. It draws out confidence and grace, rejoicing that we are more than just flesh. Even just a few minutes of walking around the trunks and tapping fingers against the grooves whispers to one's greater being. It hones in on specific fates and directs a person to discover their primary purpose, accept their fate and meet it with enthusiasm.

Where we come from and how we are formed affects this—whether we like it or not. Once a person accepts their start in this world and makes peace with the unfairness that is wrought throughout life, they can develop their unique powers and refine the abilities that follow them.

Power comes from within. How it develops is based on the abilities a person exudes and works with. Cultivating the energies that live inside ourselves requires patience. Meditation, ritual, and sometimes spellwork is necessary to draw that power out and utilize it in the physical world where the seen and unseen overlap.

One must connect to the natural world to weave individual power into able, tangible change. All creatures host a divine right to interconnection, but trees present the oldest, most profound form of spiritual intonation in known existence. They await our calls. They know us better than we often know ourselves because their consciousness is based on vibration and elemental growth.

Some spiritualists walk their path without discovering the mighty voice of the trees. Everyone has their own steps to take, but there are those of us who cannot avoid the whispering woods. I have experienced an undefined source of knowledge, understanding, and receiving ideas without needing to open a book or take a course. (Books and teachers are vital resources that have greatly influenced my life's journey, but they are just a couple of aids—there are more methods that feed a quest for knowledge).

Among the trees, I have come to find that there is no age limit to exploration. There is no end to learning. Throughout every phase of my life, the trees have been there. They stood tall when I felt cut down.

They presented balanced influences that helped guide me back toward nurturing growth.

No matter what a person experiences, they cannot avoid absorbing something from the wooded beings that support each breath. We intake their output and, with that, draw in some of their essences. It begins with the mother. Everything she breathes is filtered into our bodies before we even know how to be human.

Everything starts as a seed. All creatures must root themselves in the soil of fertility to have a chance for a future. The spirit may not yet be sparked, but the ingredients are there for those who find their way toward a nurturing path.

Parenthood is not for everyone. It is a dedication that never ends. Even when delivering a baby and relinquishing parentage, a tie is formed.

Since every story must begin, so too does the progression of magic. For spiritualists wishing to intertwine the young they are, or will be, supporting with the entirety of the world's possibilities, there are specific meditations, rites, and spells that pertain to pregnancy.

My children are my great work. They tie me to generations that will take up the gauntlet and link me back to ancestors who passed on maternal traits that aid me daily. For everyone else, flip ahead. There is a wealth of energy to be shared for any stage of life, and we all host some importance regardless of our family ties.

16

———

TREE PREGNANCY MEDITATIONS

HOW A COUPLE APPROACHES EXPANDING THEIR FAMILY AFFECTS their success. Sometimes physical limitations are involved, but mental stress can exacerbate frustrating situations. To find a better way into parenthood, there are meditations, rituals, and spells that both men and women can perform and/or practice together to better ease the mind, soothe the soul, and relax the body.

These methods are all deeply connected to humanity's connection to the world that nurtures it. The main source derives from the present link between life and air. Air and the great forests that cover the planet.

Trees are hosts of life. They give us the means to breathe and fill the world with seeds, of which many never develop. Instead of viewing this exciting time of trying for a baby as a race or competition, looking to the calm, gentle wooden giants outside my window lent me strength. It gave me what I needed to look beyond traditional medicine.

Mind over matter is more powerful than we know. Concentration and focus on a situation are proven to create more positive results. Utilizing this ability and mingling it with the spiritual world sways the universe in impossible ways.

Fertility Meditation

(Best done before conception attempt for males, and after for females)

Step 1: Find a comfortable space to relax and forget time.

Step 2: Lie down and breathe as deeply as possible while clearing the mind.

Step 3: Breathe out as slow as possible.

Step 4: Breathe out and expel all doubt, poisonous ideas, and fears.

Step 5: Breathe in and absorb the energies of life. Visualize a seed being dropped just before it takes root in the ground. Recognize the power of trusting your body, your fate, and the universe's will.

Step 6: Give in to the trust. Keep breathing in and out as slowly as possible. Let the calm fill your body. Take 100 of these breaths and be at peace with what comes.

Potential Life Rooting

(For mother, father, or couple to do together. Best done after attempted conception(s) through the first few weeks after getting a positive pregnancy test.)

Step 1: Lie in bed and breathe deeply.

Step 2: Place your hands on the womb.

Step 3: Close your eyes and visualize the fertilized egg rooting within the womb. .

Step 4: With each breath, see it growing more attached and prepared for the growth that will occur.

Grounding

(Perfect for couples to do together during the second trimester of pregnancy)

Step 1: Go outside and walk to the strongest tree in sight. The one which is the thickest, tallest, and holds the most flourishing limbs.

Step 2: Sit at the trunk, among the roots.

Step 3: Place your hands on the roots and rub them up and down. Feel the friction; the energy grow and connect you with the tree.

Step 4: Feel that energy alive within. Keep one hand on the root and place the other on the womb.

Step 5: Visualize the energy within the growing baby's rooted life source. How it draws nutrients from the soil that is the mother, and how its body grows from that source of power.

Step 6: Connect these energies. Push the vibrations or the warmth coming from the roots through your body and envision those of the new life expanding and growing to reach the tree that holds so much knowledge and wisdom.

Step 7: Hold that bond for as long as possible. A sensation of oneness should take over. The great mastery of the links that connect the entire universe may present itself. Follow the journey but keep a clear picture of yourself, the tree, and the new life in mind.

Step 8: Lie down and stare at the sky through the tree cover overhead. Place your palms downward upon the ground and release your hold on the unknown.

Step 9: Breathe deep and relax until any fogginess wears off.

Step 10: Sit up and smile at the possibilities that are everywhere.

Movement

(Once kicks are felt, the parents can do this individually or together to celebrate and encourage healthy movements)

Step 1: Sit outside on a clear day, hopefully during an awake period when the baby kicks.

Step 2: Look at the trees in the area. See how the sun touches them, how the wind tickles the leaves.

Step 3: Relax and think of the womb as the sun, the wind, and the waters that hydrate.

Step 4: Visualize the growing life within as a sapling receiving nourishment. The heat of the mother's body is the center of its solar system. The rushing blood through the body carries oxygen to immature lungs. Amniotic fluid surrounds the little one in a bubble of oceanic safety.

Step 5: If kicks occur, think of the ripples those movements create. Recognize the impact even potential life offers before birth. If not, still think of them but with more hopes for the future.

Step 6: If any words come to mind, speak, sing, or chant them to the baby. Let each syllable serve as a promise or a lullaby.

Bonding

(Individual bonding is vital for mothers. This should be done alone for the mother, but if the father wishes to do it as well, it should be done separately.)

Step 1: Go for a hike in the woods. Find a local or state park to visit and really connect with.

Step 2: Acknowledge the new energies within and how they change your mannerisms.

Step 3: It is sometimes easy to get scared or worried about changes. To calm that anxiety, study the trees along the path. See how they vary in patterns, heights, and branches.

Step 4: Breathe deeply and think back to your earliest memory. Remember growing and changing. How it was once scary to think of driving, dating, or moving out on your own.

Step 5: Now, think of your accomplishments. Smile on just living this far and being gifted the opportunity to take moments like these.

Step 6: Step aside and stop. Breathe deep. Look up. Close your eyes and smell the life surrounding you. Listen to the wind, the air

Step 7: Get back on the trail and whisper, sing, or talk to your baby as you keep going. Stop if you hear others and feel uncomfortable with them hearing, but really try to express your fears and hopes to the baby inside.

Step 8: Then, visualize the birth and cuddling the newborn in the future.

Step 9: Let the forest blanket you with a sense of peace in accepting the possibilities.

Step 10: Finish your walk and enjoy a snack or meal afterward. Repeat as often as necessary.

Nurturing Hope

(Perfect to be done individually or with both parents to look to the future with love and light)

Step 1: Sit on a porch or before an open window and glance out at the trees/plants.

Step 2: Watch the sky. Feel the wind. Breathe in the nutrients.

Step 3: Think of each breath as food for the future.

Step 4: Visualize the developing baby finishing their growth into the world.

Step 5: Think of how they will be born to look at the sky, chase the wind, and breathe in everything that comes.

Step 6: How can you, as a parent/future parent, make the world a little nicer, safer, and more loving? Think of the little things that gave childhood its happy moments for you and how you wish to pass those on to your child(ren).

Step 7: Look to the trees/plants and ask them to help you. Thank the Gods for their guidance and the hopes you hold.

Step 8: Keep your hopes close to you. Be realistic, but don't be afraid to look forward to the future with a smile.

Step 9: This is a good morning or evening routine to practice as the pregnancy nears its end. Repeating it at least once a week will lend you trust in yourself, your baby, nature, and the gods. Trust is the foundation of the love that will bind your family together as it grows and changes.

Preparing for all Skies

(For just the mother in preparation for birthing)

Step 1: Before a storm or just as one starts, find a stick and bring it inside.

Step 2: Turn off all the lights and sit in the center of the room holding the stick. Let it represent the trees that must withstand the harsher aspects of existence during rough weather.

Step 3: Listen to the outside world.

Step 4: Close your eyes and visualize the stick as an extension of the power of the forests that connects all trees and living beings.

Step 5: Now press it to your womb. Let the energies mingle. Feel the life inside you and its bond with all of creation.

Step 6: Accept that, like the stick, all things will fall, break, and go back to the earth someday.

Step 7: Think of all the happy moments you've shared during the pregnancy and what it means to you.

Step 8: Look to the last small part of gestation. See yourself going into labor and accepting the challenge the universe has tasked you with.

Step 9: Breath slowly and steadily. Listen to the storm. Hear its power, its force. Remember that, like the elements, you too, hold the energies to command and set your own course.

Step 10: Let your thoughts drift and find the words, images, or sensations that define your hope for the future. Now repeat it or hold it for as long as possible. Let the words grow louder, the picture becomes more vibrant, or the sensation expands through your body.

Step 11: Now, push yourself beyond that. Grip the stick to keep thoughts based in reality but see life rushing ahead. Know that it will end for you and, eventually, your little one. Accept the balance in the beauty/ sorrow of mortality. Open your eyes.

Step 12: Lay down with the stick. Cradle it in your arms. Once again, focus on the storm but hear the truth in it.

Step 13: Push away all fear and rub your belly. Talk to your baby-to-be. Open up about life and what you wish to experience.

Step 14: When finished, eat a snack or meal.

Step 15: Keep the stick until the storm passes and the ground is dry enough to bury or burn it in a fire pit.

Step 16: Do so at the next opportunity, meditating on what you've learned from your experiences, but keep this last round light. Just a simple short acknowledgment will do.

Standing Tall

(For the mother during Braxton hicks contractions/ practice labor, and the very earliest stage of labor)

Step 1: Stand up when contractions start.

Step 2: Breath deep and spread your feet apart at a comfortable distance.

Step 3: Rock and sway to your own rhythm while visualizing the sky above you getting ready to bestow a new day.

Step 4: Moan low, like a howling wind.

Step 5: Move and bend as needed. Remember that the strongest trees are also the most flexible.

Step 6: Continue as needed until harsher pains escalate.

17

TREE PREGNANCY RITUALS

MEDITATION IS MAINLY DRIVEN BY THE MIND. IT brings peace to the brain and helps one control their body. Ritual is more physical.

The actions and materials in a ritual give the body the items needed to further connect with the energies surrounding a person and their purpose. It further defines the need to direct energies more directly. Tree Pregnancy Rituals help to connect the mother, child, and nature for positive outcomes.

Fertility Ritual

(Best done by mother and father for increased fertility)

MATERIALS NEEDED: A pole, ribbon or streamers, an egg, and a feast of healthy foods are essential: strawberries, bananas, celery, carrots, sunflower seeds, peanuts, dried fruits, and optional lean meats and dairy

PREPARATION: Meditate to clear the mind and push away doubts or worries. Have the food ready for after the rite. The father-to-be should stick the pole in the ground, or if small-sized, in the center of a decorated altar full of signs of life: eggs, flowers, etc. Best done during Beltane.

THE WORK:

1. Have the man and woman wishing to conceive bow to each other before the pole.

2. The couple should then dance together around the ritual area, building energies for as long as they wish.

3. When ready, the father should touch the pole and whisper, chant, or sing to the male aspect of Gods for strength and virility.

4. Then he should back away, giving the mother-to-be enough space to take up a ribbon or streamer and dance around the pole to wrap it. She should then turn in the opposite direction, take up another, and repeat. This changing course and wrapping of the ribbon need only be done 4 times in a rite this small. (If during Beltane, it can be done on a grander scale with many others or a small group-if the couple in question wishes to share their hopes).

5. After wrapping the pole, the woman should walk up to it and touch it, whispering, singing, or chanting to the female aspects of the universe for nurturing power and maternal fulfillment.

6. The couple should then dance together and arouse one another, then consummate their hopes before the altar (if during a larger Beltane celebration and wishing for privacy, having a tent ready to sneak off is very appropriate).

7. Once given of each other, rest together for at least 100 deep breaths. Then feast on the healthy foods that will aid growth and familial hopes.

Seeding

(To be done any time after attempted conception through the first 6 weeks of pregnancy)

MATERIALS NEEDED: Tree seeds, a small sapling, a food offering, and fresh fruits and vegetables for afterward

PREPARATION: Obtain a tree or shrub seed(s) or sapling to plant in either a pot in the home or outside. Get fresh fruits and veggies for a small feast but also set aside something as an offering to be planted with the seeds/sapling. Best done on the full moon.

THE WORK:

1. During a full moon ritual. Meditate on the seed(s) or sapling. Visualize it growing into a robust and healthy adult plant.

2. Then focus on the potential life in the womb. Focus your thoughts and energies on nurturing that life and preparing it for the world.

3. Now set the plant where it will find fresh air and light by a window in your home, or take it outside where it will be planted.

4. During the next day, dig a hole in the pot or outside. Set the sapling or seed(s) and bury your food offering in the dirt, where its nutrients will help the plant grow.

5. Then sit before it and chant, sing, or whisper to the gods for the health and well-being of the planta and the baby, creating a deeper connection between them.

6. Stand and smile at the plant. Talk to it and the potential life if you wish. Then, feast on the fruits and vegetables to nourish the womb's atmosphere.

Sapling Growth

(Best done by mother and father during the last half of the 1st trimester)

MATERIALS NEEDED: Indoor tree or outdoor sapling already planted (see Seeding Ritual), fresh fruits, vegetables, nuts/seeds, cheeses, milk, fish or beef, preferred cleansing herb, hedge clippers, a basin of water, and single candle and matches

PREPARATION: Best done on a full moon at night. Have foods for feast ready nearby the plants. Bless the water beforehand by meditating your energies into it while dipping your fingertips along the surface. If during cold weather, a fire is customary. Do it during the full moon ritual or as your own rite.

THE WORK:

1. Place the candle directly in front of the plant, the hedge clippers

to the left of the candle, and the basin of water to the right. Light the cleansing herb and dance around the space, clearing away all negative energies.

2. Kneel before the plants and meditate on their growth. Recognize any changes, even if they are regressive, such as wilting.

3. Speak to the sapling like you would a child. Talk to it about life and ask questions if they come to you.

4. Look to the sky and sing, chant, or whisper to the Gods, thanking them for the simple ability to sit before a living plant and share your energies.

5. Then light the candle and hold it up to the sky. Let the flame dance before your eyes. Focus on it and set it gently before the tree. Close your eyes and hold your palm up to the heat. Chant, sing, or whisper to the energy it gives, and thank the light for offering nourishment to the plant and yourself. Place the same palm on the growing womb and thank the light for readying the growing baby.

6. Now take up the hedge clippers. Consecrate them by holding the metal blades over the flame, then clipping away any drying blanches, buds, or twigs from the sapling. Drop them into the basin of water.

7. Bring the bowl before the candle and gaze upon the clippings in the water. Meditate on them and their sacrifice, how all creatures must shed some "blood" or "layers" in order to survive.

8. If images appear in the water, let them speak to you.

9. Once more, take up the candle, but drip wax onto the clippings in the water. Chant, sing, or whisper words biding growth with change and sometimes pain. Hold the bowl up to the sky and thank the universe for the opportunity to nurture a growing life and for the potential to know the joys of parenting.

10. Set the candle back in front of the plant and bow to it.

11. Turn to your partner and kiss. Feast on the healthy food that will

grow a strong baby, and discuss your hopes and fears. Express them equally and end the conversation on a positive note.

Tree Spirit

(To be done during sunshine as an offering for good fortune)

MATERIALS NEEDED: Pinecones, peanut butter, birdseed, pieces of colored string, and healthy foods for a small feast.
PREPARATION: To be done outside on a sunny day.

THE WORK:
1. Take a walk and collect pinecones.
2. Bring the pinecones home and make natural bird feeders by coating them in natural peanut butter and then rolling them in bird seed. Wrap string around the top level of the openings on the cone until secure, then tie it, so it is ready to be hung in a tree. An organic string is best, as the birds can also use it in their nests once the pinecone breaks down.
3. Go outside, carry the basket of pinecone bird feeders, and walk among the trees closest to your home. Think of all the life they support, how many animals and insects need these great giants to survive.
4. Imagine the needs of young creatures and how your child will require your support once it is born.
5. Visualize this need as you hang the birdfeeders. One by one, let your thoughts connect you to the laws of life. It is not always fair, but it gives everyone completion, which balances everything.
6. Once hung, stand before the offerings. Chant, sing, or whisper and

circle around the area (dance if the mood speaks of it), repeating words of thanks for the life you lead and the chance to share your knowledge directly with the next generation.

7. Find the gratitude inside and give thanks to the Gods for the opportunity. Even if all does not go well, hope has a distinct power over humanity.

8. Then feast on a light meal of healthy fruits, nuts, etc.

9. Save any leftovers to compost and return to the earth during the next full moon.

Watering Needs

(To increase health/growth)

MATERIALS NEEDED: A water filter, freshwater spring, or clean bottled water. Towel(s). Healthy foods for a light feast.
PREPARATION: Ready the feast. Be near the water.

THE WORK:

1. Stand before the water and bow to it. Meditate on the necessity, how our bodies and our planet are mostly made of water.

2. Now dip your hands into the spring or pour the water into your palm. Hold it over the womb and let the water run over it, dripping down the curvature.

3. Breath deep. Envision the cool water as a life source, the true Fountain of Youth.

4. Now drink some of the water. Feel it rush through your body. Imagine it reaching through your limbs as if to root you into this world.

5. Visualize the trees that absorb the rain. Their role in slurping up flood waters and pollution. Recognize your role in that and chant, sing, or whisper to provide your child with a clean future.

6. Drink in purity. Speak to yourself, your unborn child, and the Gods of the hydration that is life.

7. If at a spring, then walk into the water and splash about. Let it revive you.

8. Dry off if needed, then drink the water while feasting on healthy fruits, veggies, nuts, and optional cheeses and meats.

Maternal Voice

(To better bond with your unborn baby)

MATERIALS NEEDED: Potted plant or outdoor space under a tree with protruding roots. Healthy snacks like homemade trail mix, and a jar of water.

PREPARATION: Sit in the sunshine with a potted plant or at the foot of the tree and meditate on the moment. Clear away all outside thoughts. Pull focus to the here and now instead of the past or future.

THE WORK:

1. Gently place fingertips along roots. (If using a potted plant, carefully dig until touching.)

2. Breathe in deeply and close your eyes.

3. Place the other hand at the womb.

4. Feel the power of the roots. How they are the main vessel of communication for plants.

5. Instead of relying on vocalization, feel the root of your child and let that energy connect to you on a higher level. Your pulse, your breathing, everything you are is a part of this little creature's well-being. Utilize that power and control your breathing. Centralize your emotions with your physical being and let them vibrate together.

6. What do you wish to pass on to your child? What life lessons do you know will benefit them throughout life? Speak of them now, but do not just rely on the power of your voice. Be aware of your posture, breathing, and sensations that arise at the mere mention of certain topics.

7. Speak to the growing life within you as if they understand everything. Do not hold back or worry about anyone hearing.

8. Enjoy the day and talk as much as you wish, drinking when your voice is dry and munching on your snack when the appetite calls for it.

9. Repeat this as often as comfort allows.

Cultivating a Nursery

(To prepare for your baby during the 3rd trimester)

MATERIALS NEEDED: A branch full of fresh leaves or pine needles

PREPARATION: Cut a fresh branch to consecrate a nursery with the wisdom of the woods. Thank the tree for its sacrifice.

THE WORK:

1. Prepare the nursery. Have furniture built and placed where it suits best, along with decorations, toys, and even clothing.

2. Bring in the branch and stand in the doorway with it. Chant, whis-

per, or sing, asking for the nursery to sprout happy, healthy moments for the baby once it arrives.

3. Hold the branch out and walk around the room, waving it over every area of the room. Visualize your child growing strong, ready to walk tall in the world.

4. Make a full circle, then come back to the doorway and bow.

5. Burn the branch in a ritual fire on the next full moon or holiday.

Patience in Discomfort

(To gain patience as you await labor)

MATERIALS NEEDED: Basket

PREPARATION: Grab a basket to gather leaves, berries, sticks, nuts, and twigs.

THE WORK:

1. Take a walk among the trees. Be aware of the limits of late pregnancy. Acknowledge pains, but go as far as possible to ease the discomfort and restlessness.

2. Listen to the sounds within the area. Stop when needed.

3. Collect odd-looking leaves, sticks, or berries—those that are misshapen or broken.

4. At the end of the walk, go over these strange pieces of nature. Hold them, feel for them. Even in their condition, they still serve a purpose.

5. Meditate on this. As changed as a mother is before giving birth, she is not deformed or broken, yet sometimes feels as if she is.

6. Let the trees refresh the mind and the air sing with the truth.

7. Breathe in the necessity of the last and most frustrating stage of pregnancy and take pride in surviving its hardship. Now chant, sing, or whisper something to the effect that peace can be found beyond discomfort. Time is coming.

Strong as Wood

(To aid the mother through labor)

MATERIALS NEEDED: Comfortable room, focal point, soothing music or background noise, whatever eases the mother, water or tea, applesauce, or other easy soft food.

PREPARATION: Have everything ready for when labor begins. If going to a birthing center or hospital, have bags packed and ready. If home-birthing, prepare a kit as advised by a midwife or aid.

THE WORK:

1. When labor begins, remain calm and thank the gods for getting you this far.

2. Get up, and move around. Play music. Watch a movie. Do whatever passes the time in the early stage of labor. It is okay if the pain isn't cinematic or the water doesn't break immediately. The water will break when it is ready, and most of the heavy pains come after it is broken, so do not be eager to have it burst.

3. Standing through the early contractions helps move the process along faster. It gets the baby further down in position and opens the cervix. Sitting and lying down is less helpful. To get in the proper mindset, imagine you are as strong as wood. A solid tree withstanding a wildfire.

4. Hum, sing, whisper, or chant of your strength and that of your baby. Be prepared for anything. Nothing is guaranteed but focus on getting through each moment and centering yourself.

5. Take small sips of water or tea if possible, and even small bites of simple foods like applesauce will offer energy when it wanes throughout the last phase.

6. As time progresses, give in to your body. Let it guide you.

7. The fire will die down, and the heat will pass. Focus on doing what is needed and getting to the end.

19

TREE PREGNANCY SPELLS

FROM CONCEPTION THROUGH DELIVERY, THERE ARE SPELLS THAT help hone personal energies to nurture and protect a pregnancy. The parent(s) must be fully committed. A spell cast as an only effort is less potent. Those who dedicate themselves completely, working to live healthy, think healthy, and breathe healthily, are more likely to harbor the true powers necessary to sway the universe and its outcomes.

Growing a healthy baby takes patience. It also requires faith and love. When ready to offer these aspects of oneself without question, these spells provide aid and results. They are the physical prayers that speak directly to the world.

Fertility Spell

(To enhance fertility)

MATERIALS NEEDED: An egg, bowl of food scraps, foot of a tree or garden

PREPARATION: Collect leftovers and food scraps in a bowl for at least a week before the rite, if not one moon cycle. This will be an offering to the earth's energies. Just before the rite, meditate on conception, or if aiding a loved one, on their conceiving.

THE WORK:

1. Carry the bowl to the outdoor garden or the foot of a tree between roots. Kneel and set the bowl down.
2. Place hands over the leftovers and envision them returning to the earth as an offering. If compelled to do so, chant or sing.
3. Dig a hole large enough for the food offering and place the leftovers into the soil, leaving the hole open.
4. When ready, take the egg in your hands. Hold over the bowl and visualize a healthy creature forming without complications.
5. Bring the egg close to your heart and rock it as if it were a baby. Kiss it. Welcome protection and guidance for the life that is to be.
6. Crack the egg over the food offering in the soil. Crush the shell with your hands and place it beside the egg atop the food.
7. Cover with dirt while envisioning a healthy new life. It may take up to a month to fulfill, but it should come to be.
8. Bow to the earth and thank it for its power. Then lay back and ground the body. Feel the energies wane and rebalance. Any lightheadedness should dissipate. The body should feel relaxed.

Healthy Maternity Spell

(For the mother to do with the father or on her own during the first 6 weeks of pregnancy)

MATERIALS NEEDED: lemon (sliced in 2 halves), lavender flowers or oil, preferred cleansing herb, strawberries and cup of whole milk, small garden shovel

PREPARATION: Perform during the waxing moon cycle to attract positive outcomes during day, preferably in the sunshine under a familiar tree or at least with a potted plant.

THE WORK:

1. Place items before the space and burn the preferred cleansing herb, walking clockwise, then counterclockwise in a circle around the tree or plant.

2. Stand in the sun or a warm space and close your eyes. Feel the energy within you. Build it from the base of your being throughout your limbs. Let it stretch beyond.

3. Take the lemon and bite into one half, sucking in the juices. Take the other half and rub it on the womb, singing, chanting, or whispering of the healing power of the sun and its most potent citrus fruit. Set aside.

4. Take up the lavender and rub the oil or flowers on the womb, again chant, sing, or whisper of the healing power of plants and nature's most forgiving flower. Set aside.

5. Sit beneath the tree and take up a strawberry in one hand and the milk in another. Look to the tree and above. Acknowledge the endless wisdom of the sky. Thank the universe for providing the elements to aid life and progress.

6. Look upon the strawberry and acknowledge its nutrients. Within each berry is stored folic acid, a primary necessity for growing a healthy life. Take a bite and revel in the flavor.

7. Sip the milk and appreciate its ability to build stronger bones and give young the fat necessary to regulate body heat.

8. Finish the snack but save one strawberry and a small sip of milk.

Bury the strawberry stems under the tree, placing the whole one on top as an offering. Pour the milk on top, sing, chant, or whisper your wish for a healthy pregnancy.

9. Bow to the tree, bow to the universe, and bow to yourself and the life that is starting its journey.

Finding Fate

(Water scrying to see future outcomes of pregnancy/parenting)

MATERIALS NEEDED: Basin of water, tree

PREPARATION: Carry a basin of water to the tree

THE WORK:

1. Gather leaves that have fallen or pluck 9 from the tree.

2. Kneel before the roots and hold the leaves close. Clear your mind.

3. Focus energies on connecting with the power of the tree's wisdom and its connection to the Gods.

4. Sprinkle the leaves into the basin and let them fall as they may. Some may not even go into the bowl. That's okay.

5. Now place one hand on the womb and the other just over the leaves floating on the water's surface.

6. Breathe deep and follow the leaf patterns. Look to the water and open your senses.

7. If patterns form, pay attention to them and explore them. If ideas materialize, let them carry your thoughts.

8. If nothing sparks, dip your fingertip in water and swirl it around.

Look to the ripples and watch the leaves spin. Ask them questions. Wait patiently.

9. Once you lose focus, bow to the tree and ground yourself.

10. Stay encouraged if nothing surfaces right away. Sometimes the answers come later.

Truth in Trust

(To increase faith in yourself, your baby, and the Gods)

MATERIALS NEEDED: Pen, paper, small garden shovel, tree or plant

PREPARATION: Go before a familiar tree outside or potted plant on the full moon or during the waxing cycle.

THE WORK:

1. Meditate on the tree or plant. Think of its life cycle and all it took to grow to be what it currently is.

2. Now think of your own life. Meditate on the similarities, how a person forms from a small creature to grow through nurturing, light and dark, storms, etc.

3. Write down the main struggles you have suffered and overcome. Anything that remains a strong memory or helped define direction or changes in your life along the way.

4. Flip the paper over. List the qualities that helped you through these times. At the bottom, write the baby's name or potential names if still being decided. If unsure, sketch a picture of the fetus or pregnant form

to represent the baby.

5. Whisper, chant, or sing about putting more trust in yourself. If compelled, get up and dance around the plant or move as you feel necessary.

6. Whisper, chant, or sing about putting trust in your body. As before, move as needed.

7. Repeat again of putting trust in the baby. Move as needed.

8. Repeat once more, and really vocalize putting trust in the gods. Let any fear of fate be absolved. Know, acknowledge, and appreciate that nothing is guaranteed but that you will find your way no matter what happens.

9. Bury the paper before the tree or in the pot. Then bury and place your hands on top to ground yourself.

Uprooting Mother Earth Within

(Spell to connect with ancestors to prepare for parenthood)

MATERIALS NEEDED: Altar, pictures and items from mother, grandmother, great-grandmother, or as far back as possible (a list of names works as well), 2-3 white candles (1-2 carved to represent the Gods, and 1 to represent journey into motherhood)

PREPARATION: Set the altar with the gods' candle at the north end and the motherhood candle at the south, with the items placed around and between.

THE WORK:

1. Sit, stand, or kneel before the altar and light to gods' candle, whispering, chanting, or singing to welcome their energies closer.

2. Pick up the candle and move it over the pictures and items slowly, one by one. Focus on any memories you have of these women who came before you.

3. Meditate on their warmth and love, their discipline and rules. Take your time.

4. Put the candle back and close your eyes. Visualize yourself as a mother. Draw from the power of these women and let your instincts come to the surface. Like a tree sucking nutrients from the ground, envision yourself drawing the lessons passed down to you so you can pass them on when the time comes.

5. Now light the motherhood candle. Chant, whisper, or sing of mother earth and her connection to the women who led to you, then bring it to a close with words of bridging those traditions and making some of your own to guide the life you are tending.

6. Ground yourself by recalling your favorite and funniest moments with the women in your family, your partner's family, or friends if family is a sore subject.

Patience from the Pines

(Spell to increase patience and understanding of pregnancy)

MATERIALS NEEDED: Pinecones, pine needles, and a pine

branch

PREPARATION: Take a walk where the pines grow and collect pinecones, needles, and a small branch or large twig with needles still attached.

THE WORK:

1. Find the largest pine tree in the area and sit beneath it with items.
2. Take up the pinecone and breathe in its scent. Feel the rough bark. Now consider how ever great pine that towers above began as a single seed— one of many— inside a pinecone.
3. Hold the pinecone up to the womb and whisper, chant, or sing of its power. Then hold it up to the sky and ask the universe to protect your womb as the cone protects its seeds.
4. Now take up a handful of pine needles. Sniff their natural fragrance. Ponder their color and makeup. Meditate on the many pine needles that cover a single adult pine.
5. Sprinkle the needles over the womb and whisper, chant, or sing of their strength. Like eyelashes, they protect the "eyes" of the pines; like hair, they keep the tree sheltered.
6. Now stand and shake off the needles. Look to the sky and hold your arms out. Ask the Gods to lend you the strength needed to protect.
7. Grab the branch. Bend down and brush the ground with it, then slowly rise up and bring it from your feet, up above your head. Think of the time and energy needed for a great pin to mature.
8. Brush the branch over the tree trunk and feel your connection to the tree as it stands before the world sheltering newer generations.
9. Whisper, chant, or sing asking the universe to lend you the secrets of patience that come with time. If compelled to do so, dance or jump about. Enjoy the sensations created by this spell. Laugh, smile, have fun, and be brave.

10. When finished, leave the branch at the foot of the tree and bow.

Bonding Through Growth

(For mother to bond with unborn child)

MATERIALS NEEDED: Olive oil, comfortable spot
PREPARATION: Have a nice block of time set aside.

THE WORK:

1. Pour a small amount of olive oil into a small container or shallow cup.

2. Gently dip your fingertips along the surface and close your eyes. Feel the source of your energy at your core and let it build through your body until it warms your limbs and spreads into the olive oil through your fingertips. It may help to imagine your energy as a light.

3. Drizzle olive oil into your palm. Rub it between your hands, again building more energy.

4. Then lie back and rub the olive oil on the womb, taking time to massage it into the skin. This will ease any itching or discomfort from growth by allowing bonding with the baby.

5. Chant, sing, or whisper your wishes for the growing being.

6. Relax and just talk to the little thing as if it were already born and listening intently.

7. When tired of speaking, smile at your belly and rest. Taking a nap is recommended.

Swaying Toward Labor

(To aid with false-labor pains or Braxton Hicks contractions)

MATERIALS NEEDED: Familiar area with trees

PREPARATION: Do in the later stages when pregnancy becomes cramped and uncomfortable on a windy day.

THE WORK:

1. Walk around the tree(s) clockwise, then counterclockwise.

2. Breathe in deeply and push out the air in a low tone. This prepares one for labor as lower, slow tones aid with pain.

3. Stand in the center of the trees or before the single tree. Wait for a gust of wind and look up. See the boughs shake.

4. Now close your eyes. Repeat this breathing, but when the next gust of wind comes, feel it, hear its voice among the trees.

5. Let those sensations influence your body. Feel your life source, the main point where your energy comes from, and let it build. Let it growl and soften with the wind.

6. Sway with the trees without having to watch them. Keep breathing and feel your sense of self grow. Let yourself revel in your own power over your body and your future.

7. Open your eyes and focus on the sky. Chant, sing, or whisper of that power and how it battles pain and uncertainty.

8. Spin or dance in the wind. Laugh and be glad for life.

Baby's Blessing

(To welcome the new baby and bless them with grace)

MATERIALS NEEDED: 5 candles (1 to represent the Gods/ Masculine aspects of life, 1 to represent the Goddesses/Feminine aspects of life, 3 for traits to be bestowed, based colors off of those chosen qualities=yellow for happiness, pink for beauty, or white all-purpose candles with symbols carved into them also work), baby's items such as booties, handmade toys, or blankets, also bells or instruments for a drum circle, food, and drink for feast afterward.

PREPARATION: Invite family and/or supportive friends. This is to be a joyous occasion, much like a Christening. Set an altar or table with the Godslife candles at the north end. Determine what 3 main traits the child will grow best with: happiness, intelligence, good health, generosity, beauty, talent, or other positive qualities, and arrange the candles with one at the east end, one at the south, and one at the west. Meditate on the candles to visualize the power of the traits and transfer energy into the candles. Place the baby's objects and other items in the center. Have food arranged and readied before starting the ceremony.

THE WORK:

1. Welcome all guests and the gods/energies while lighting the godslife candles.

2. Hold the baby up to the altar and chant about the gifts chosen.

3. With the help of your partner, hold up each candle and light them individually, chanting, praying, or singing about the purpose of each.

4. Gently bring each candle over the child's head, but be careful not to spill hot wax.

5. Have siblings and other parent ring their bells.

6. Engage everyone willing in a drum circle. Have them gather around the baby and walk or dance in a circle building their energies. When the electricity for the movement is at its height, instruct everyone to turn to the baby and send that energy to the baby.

7. Leave the candles to burn out and share a feast celebrating the new life and its blessing.

8. Keep leftovers and scraps. Gather them together and bury them at the foot of the strongest tree surrounding your home or in the garden. Chant of the offering being given for the child.

9. Bow to the earth and ground self by touching the tree, stalk, or dirt and focusing on its direct connection to the present. Let it absorb excess energies.

TREE PARENTING POWER

WHEN SEEKING GUIDANCE, TREES OFFER A SENSE OF calm. They stand before us as symbols of patience and wisdom. Like loving grandparents and wise mothers and fathers, they shelter us but leave space for growth. There is a lot that young parents can learn from trees.

It is easy to give in to protective instincts. There are many dangers in the world, but if parents shield their kids too much, these young people will not be able to handle failure or pain. Too much space can also cause issues. Children raised without any structure or discipline struggle to lead productive and compassionate lives in later years.

Leading by example is the best way to connect with young minds.

Standing tall and listening to the wind better prepares people for raising children. It is easier for an underdeveloped brain to watch someone do something and replicate it than it is for them to be told what to do without any kind of proof or hands-on learning.

I could never have succeeded in any field without experiments. Seeing, touching; feeling the world around me has led to more knowledge than any other lessons.

Like the trees, I need to root myself in an idea and build a strong foundation above it, then branch out and see how far the information and materials can go. As a child, I struggled because of a lack of structure in my home life, but nature gave me the support I needed.

Offering balance to my own children is a life-long goal. It is a never-ending struggle that seesaws up and down. Instead of being over-protective, I wish to teach my children how to look after themselves because I know that I will not be here forever, and if that happens soon and suddenly, I need them to be able to handle anything that comes their way.

Instead of stepping back and letting my kids run wild, I must also give them boundaries. They can test them as they please, but even forests cannot reach across canyons. Magic and spirituality are important elements of parenting. Learning to accept the unseen and ascend from our mortality to guide inquiring minds hosts more energy than the sun and the moon combined.

It is a lot to handle at times. No matter how mature or fit for the situation, there will be times when the tasks of parenting grow too tricky. I know I inherited my father's Irish temper. I've worked extremely hard to ensure I remain in control of myself so my children don't know the fear I did.

I've been abandoned and left to fend for myself. After having to support myself through my senior year of high school, I spent years working to find the right path. When I stepped into the role of motherhood, I placed a lot of expectations on myself. Some were unrealistic, others honored by the Gods, and as time passes, I adjust to keep needs met and compromise when situations call for it.

Standards are important so long as they are realistic. Kids absorb everything. They're so much brighter than anyone gives them credit for. They stand through whatever storms come to stunt their growth. They host the power to withstand anything if nourished with love.

Making sure that we, as parents, offer the proper mix of space, shelter, and tending is like raising a tree. Our offspring are the plants of the future. Utilizing the energies within to follow meditations, rituals, and spells for balance, guidance, and passing on important elements is not only helpful but also perfectly natural.

Tree Parenting Meditations encourage self-care. They can lead to more confident decisions as well as stronger bonds. In uncertain times they serve as a calming practice to soothe emotions and ease spiritual shifts. There are some to include children to help them connect with their spiritual side. This provides a hereditary link to the inner voice that grows strongest in adolescence.

Tree Parenting Rituals host the necessary actions to honor life and allow for consistency. The family coven solidifies with each shared rite, many of which are for the entire family. They weave stronger links and bind energies for greater purposes.

Last, Tree Parenting Spells come in a variety of forms. Since spellwork is often very personal, there are those meant for solitary casting and those that incorporate partners and/or children. How a parent presents their beliefs is up to them. Trusting your instincts and flourishing as a being and family member is most important.

19

TREE PARENTING
MEDITATIONS

D EEP BREATHING AND OTHER MEDITATION TECHNIQUES
CAN MAKE a disaster into a learning experience. Getting
up before the kids to meditate offers perspective in the
stillness. Taking a moment in the bathroom in the middle
of the day allows solitude when drowning in the needs of others.
Nighttime talks or cuddles lead to strong bonds and honest connections, but those are just a few of the little things that nurture a parent
when they are wilting.

More involved practices like pushing against a tree, pressing one's
back against a sturdy trunk, and sitting with children when they are
ready to climb into the boughs of adventure increase personal power.
They remind us that no matter how hectic life gets, there will always
be moments of balance. Meditations that correlate tree energy and
parenting can increase this peace.

Banishing Fear for the Young Meditation

(To combat fears for your child)

Step 1: Stand before your child(ren) as they sleep. Take in the peaceful scene.

Step 2: Breathe deeply and slip out of the room. Close the door and place your hands on it. Close your eyes and visualize yourself as a child. Remember the dreams and nights that come to mind.

Step 3: Now, think of how you developed over the years. How you grew and branched out.

Step 4: Open your senses and see the tree of life forming for each child. The possibilities are stronger than any harm that could present itself. Focus on that energy. Allow your "sheltering tree" power to reach out and transform your fears into a guiding shadow that guides the way.

Step 5: If possible, step outside and take in the image of a nearby tree or do so before a window.

Growing an Attentive Mindset

(To better connect with your child)

Step 1: Take a walk through a wooded park or forest area with your child(ren).

Step 2: Let them talk and focus your mind on their little thoughts.

Step 3: Now ask them to walk in silence for a short while, to listen to the trees and really pay attention to the birds, squirrels, and creatures that inhabit them

Step 4: Stop before the biggest tree you can find and have them go before it. Ask them what they hear and what they feel? Encourage a stronger sense of connection.

Step 5: Place your hands on the tree and gaze up. Ask them to join you. Breathe deep and release your energies; reach out for the tree in spirit. Describe what you feel, what you sense and hear, and why it matters to you.

Step 6: Repeat as often as desired.

"Me Time" Meditation

(To empower yourself as a parent and caretaker)

Step 1: Wake up before everyone in your home. Go outside and sit under a familiar tree facing the sun/sunrise.

Step 2: Breathe deep and clear your mind. Raise your arms up at your side when you inhale, then lower them as you exhale.

Step 3: Now, focus on what you wish to achieve for the day. Visualize yourself doing it.

Step 4: Focus on what you wish to help your child(ren) achieve. See them completing the task(s).

Step 5: Relax and let your mind wander back to yourself and the calm needed to aid you throughout your day. Let the solitude wrap around you. Appreciate it and the sheltering spirit of the tree.

Fertilizing the Day

Step 1: When waking, make coffee, tea, or just grab a glass of water and go stand before a tree outside. A porch or deck is fine, or the grass is also suitable.

Step 2: Slowly sip the drink and relax your mind. Push out all the concerns for the day and the pressures from the past. Look at the tree and breathe deeply. Watch its branches and look to the sky cradling them above.

Step 3: Keep your thoughts from flooding. Remain focused on the simple pleasure of nourishing your body and admiring the tree's example.

Step 4: When the cup is almost drained, save the last sip from the ground. Stare down into it. See if any images are drawn forth for the day. There may be hidden insights waiting at the bottom.

Step 5: Dump the rest of the drink onto the ground and imagine it drawing you and the tree together, sharing your peace and your ability to step into the day with renewed energy.

Meditating for Emotional Control

(To balance emotions and grow in peace)

Step 1: When recognizing your emotions are out of control or your child(ren)[TB1]'s emotions are, raise your arms up to the sky/have the child do it with you. Then lower them and go outside.

Step 2: Stand before the closest tree to your home and raise your arms again. Now tell yourself or your child to look at the tree and express what is causing the distress.

Step 3: Lower your arms and sit down. Close your eyes. Think of the issue and how you or your child can grow around it or past it. Discuss this or explore it in thought.

Step 4: Press your palms into the ground and look up. Breathe deep and let the calm of the natural world calm the moment. Lay down, laugh, smile, and let go of the negative electricity that built up inside.

Trimming a Temper

(To reduce anger and frustration in a heated parenting moment)

Step 1: Go outside. Get away from the confines of walls and roofing. Separate yourself from what set you off as soon as possible.

Step 2: March up to a trusted tree. Plant your feet and press your palms against the trunk, then lean in, pushing with all your force.

Step 3: Visualize your anger being driven from your body as you physically exert yourself against the immovable tree. Release it into the bark. Allow the tension to release your weight.

Step 4: Step back and shake your arms. Bow your head and breathe deep. Think of what is bothering you. Explore if there are further depths than what comes to mind. Are there underlying issues that remain unresolved?

Step 5: Look at the tree and stand tall with it. Recognize that everyone gets angry, but part of self-awareness is keeping control even when we feel uprooted or dislodged. Breathe deep and remain outside until reasoning is fully regained.

Strengthening Roots Meditation with Children

(To draw deeper connections with your heritage and pass on familial wisdom)

Step 1: Go to a tree nearby home and kneel before it. Breathe deep together.

Step 2: Have everyone close their eyes, and from youngest to oldest, say their name and who they are. (Let them define themselves how they will)

Step 3: Now, as the adult facilitator, describe the generations that came before and how their spirits/influence stand over the family and connect everyone like the very roots of the trees beneath everyone.

Step 4: Instruct everyone to focus on this truth and explore the connections between the past, the present, and the future.

Step 5: After ample time, let everyone express what they experienced one by one going from eldest to youngest. Have fun talking about it.

Swaying with Peace

(To reduce stress within the family)

Step 1: After a hectic day during windy weather, go just outside your home by the nearest tree alone or with your family.

Step 2: Breathe deep. Clear your mind, and sway with the boughs overhead. Look to the trees and rock in time.

Step 3: Let all the day's stress fall from you as if shedding weak twigs and sticks.

Step 4: Clasp your hands in front of you or join hands with the group. Close your eyes and sway, focusing on blowing away unwanted thoughts and frustrations. Let the clear air fill your lungs and revive your spirit.

Nurturing the Spirit Meditation with Children

(Increasing children's personal power and better connect the family)

Step 1: Sit in a circle with your family under a favorite tree.

Step 2: Have everyone breathe deeply and look up. Instruct all to close their eyes and still envision the tree.

Step 3: Have them visualize themselves as the tree with their family surrounding them. Go around and ask each person how they feel from youngest to oldest. If they feel silly, laugh with them, and have fun with it.

Step 4: Have the family open their eyes and stand together. Clasp hands and bow heads. Breathe deeply together and close eyes once more

Step 5: Tell everyone to let the energy inside grow with a bright, happy light and to send it out through their hands to everyone in the circle.

Step 6: Ask everyone to express how they feel, one by one, from oldest to youngest. Then raise hands and open eyes. Release grasps and step back. Look to the tree once more and tell everyone to have fun.

20

TREE PARENTING
RITUALS

S OMETIMES WE FORGET WHO WE ARE. PRESSURE FORCES us into disarray when working to be good parents. Stresses come and go, but how we handle ourselves during the worst times is what children remember most.

Ritual provides routine breaks while also offering a practice to look forward to. Instead of pushing down our frustrations, a ritual takes all the negative energy and allows us to transform it into fuel for a better outcome. Sometimes this is best done individually, whereas other times, inviting children and/or other family members and friends increases the event's effects. These Tree Parenting Rituals are the basis for many helpful familial events.

Celebrating Parenthood

(Ritual to honor your role and accept it wholeheartedly)

MATERIALS NEEDED: 1 white ribbon for each parent and child, 1 black ribbon for each parent and child, as well as the tree, and milk or water for each participant

PREPARATION: Best done when a new baby is young or after an adoption.

THE WORK:

1. Take the ribbons and drinks and set them before a familiar tree.
2. Have the parent(s) tie the black ribbon to the child's (ren's) left wrist and the white ribbon to the right. While doing so, chant, sing, or whisper of the powers of balance bringing you closer together, and speak of how there will be good and bad times, but as a parent, you will always do your best to be fair and just.
3. The parent(s) should tie their ribbons on their wrists. Can help each other as needed. Once bound, have the parent(s) sing, chant, or whisper of their dedication to their child(ren).
4. All participants should now put their hands together and bow their heads. Let the energies mingle.
5. Stand tall, thank the universe for these moments, and drink a toast to a family tree that stands firm yet caring.

Honoring Roots

MATERIALS NEEDED: A picture of your mother, father, grandmother, grandfather, and so on as far back as possible, a trusted tree, a single white candle, and matches.

PREPARATION: If doing this with a partner, include pictures of their parents, grandparents, and so on, as well as a second candle.

THE WORK:

1. Kneel before the tree and set the pictures up against the foot of the trunk.

2. Meditate on the images and how the people in them made you who you are today. Look from the tree's roots all the way up to the branches overhead and let your energies build.

3. Place the candle between yourself and the pictures. Chant, sing, or whisper of the energy that connects us all, how your family has grown and how you intend to pass on the torch.

4. Meditate on the candle's flame. Focus on your lineage, those who paved the way for you. Let the spirits speak if willing.

5. When exhausted, thank the Gods. Blow out the candle and bow to the tree. Gather up the photos and ground yourself.

Ritual to Tend Trunks

(Strengthening your parental duty and confidence)

MATERIALS NEEDED: A large stick (one for each person if multiple people are participating), a familiar tree

PREPARATION: Charge the stick with your energies by meditating on the object and visualizing the power within you pouring into the stick.

THE WORK:

1. Stand before the tree facing north.

2. Hold the stick vertically in line with your belly button and sternum. Focus on the strength of the trunk before you. Meditate on it and its continued force.

3. Bring the stick up in front of your face, still vertical in line with your nose. Close your eyes and breathe deep. Visualize your growth as a person and a parent.

4. Open your eyes and raise the stick as high as possible. Now look up and call upon the Gods to help you continue expanding balance on your journey.

5. Think of any hardships hindering your ability to be a strong, successful parent. Bring the stick end to the ground, still in line with your body, ideally in front of the space between your legs.

6. Place enough pressure on the stick so that you can circle it, and it will support some of your weight, but not too much. Walk in a circle with the stick as your gravitational center. Chant, sing, or whisper about staying true to your core, trunk, and innermost self.

7. When exhausted, place the stick beneath the tree, bow to it, and go

on your way, recharged and strengthened inside and out.

Offering Courage During Growth

(To aid through childhood changes or new family stages)

MATERIALS NEEDED: Preferred cleansing herb, matches, trusted tree, two handfuls of pebbles, rocks, or stones/gems (preferably collected by yourself), a pile of twigs

PREPARATION: Best done one-on-one with parent and child when having trouble accepting changes that come with growth and new stages of life.

THE WORK:

1. Go before the tree and set up a small makeshift altar placing the twigs in a fair-sized triangle with the topmost point facing the sun. Place the stones beneath the triangle and cleanse the triangle calling on the elements to honor your workings.

2. Now have the individual needing courage to sit before the triangle holding the stones between both hands. Clear the mind and focus all energies on connecting with the power of the compressed earth.

3. Take the largest rock/stone/etc., and place it in the center of the triangle. Speak of it representing the spirit in its wholeness.

4. Now take the medium rocks and lay them out around it in a coil. Speak of this pattern representing the growth that is needed to find one's way.

5. Lay out the smaller rocks, coiling them from largest to smallest. Speak of childhood and its many stages.

6. When all the rocks are set in a great coil that wraps around the largest stone, hold your hands over it and meditate on the wonders and terrors of maturing. Vocalize fears and hopes, curiosity and disgust.

7. Then raise your hands to the sky and ask for the courage to tackle this stage and the rest. Clasp hands with the child and meditate on this purpose.

8. Stand and bow to each other. Don't be afraid to laugh, joke, or dance about childishly.

9. Leave the coil as a symbol of purpose and direction in times of uncertainty.

Rite to Reduce Stress

(To remember your parenting strengths and the importance of your family)

MATERIALS NEEDED: Small pieces of paper, pen, candle, matches, fire-safe bowl, and tree

PREPARATION: Best done during a waning moon cycle

THE WORK:

1. Go before a tree and kneel. Whisper, chant, or sing of your need to reduce stress, and ask the gods to aid you through the power of the great wooden giant.

2. Place the candle before you and the fire-safe bowl behind it. Now light the candle calling for the elements to offer comfort.

3. Write each parental issue weighing you down on a small piece of paper, one at a time.

4. Now stand and hang the papers on the tree, poking them onto the ends of branches like seeds or children waiting.

5. Step back and marvel at the greatness of the tree. Now walk in a circle focusing on the stress and how it affects you and your connection to your family. Turn and walk in a circle in the opposite direction and visualize solutions.

6. Now remove each paper one by one. Sit before the candle and state your purpose and how you plan to overcome the issues. Light them on fire and place them in the bowl.

7. Blow out the candle and bow to the tree when all is burned. Thank the Gods and be free.

Finding Tree Circles to Ward off Fears

(Ritual to combat fears for your children and family)

MATERIALS NEEDED: A walking stick for each participant (find while performing)

PREPARATION: Best done during the waning moon cycle

THE WORK:

1. Take a walk through the forest and clear your mind. Open your senses and observe the beauty surrounding you.

2. Find a stick that calls to you. It must be large enough to function as a walking stick. Everyone present needs to find one.

3. Utilize the walking stick, thumping it in time with your steps. As this rhythm increases, extend your energies. Let the power inside warm your body and reach the stick. Push that electricity into it.

4. Scan the scenery as you walk along. Look for tree circles: a cluster of trees shaped into a ring or a tree that has split and grown up into multiple trunks that circle their origin. Step into the center of the tree ring. (If there is not enough room for everyone, do the steps individually.)

5. Close your eyes and get comfortable. Feel the encompassing life of the tree(s) wrap around you. Take in the closeness, the protective energy.

6. Now vocalize your fears for your family and yourself (one by one, if in a group).

7. Open your eyes and raise your stick. Let it reach as high as possible, like the trees. Pour all the anxiety and worry into your walking stick and send it out through the tip. Chant, sing, or whisper of banishing these fears.

8. Lower the stick. Bow to it, then toss it away. Thank the trees and leave the circle.

Finding Truth in the Leaves Ritual

(To seek the future of your family)

MATERIALS NEEDED: Collection of leaves and a friendly tree
PREPARATION: Best done in the fall. Collect a basket of leaves and meditate on it. Connect your parental energies to the contents.

THE WORK:

1. Sit under a tree with your back to the trunk facing west at sunset.

2. Take up the basket and welcome the elements in the name of family. Then spill the contents before you. Let them fall where they may.

3. Close your hands and pick up one leaf. Relax your mind and think of your child(ren). Feel the texture of the leaf and let its power influence your thoughts.

4. Open your eyes and study the leaf. Does it resemble anyone? Does it host a pattern that brings forward answers or wisdom? It's okay if not, but be open to the energies.

5. Repeat this process for as long as needed. Then focus on the overall picture/pattern of the leaves left before you. Again, relax and allow the leaves to "speak" as they please.

6. When exhausted, sit back and gaze at the sky. Press your hands against the earth and appreciate what is before you.

Spreading the Seeds of Knowledge Rite

(To be done at Samhain, Yule, or during the new moon cycle for passing on family lessons)

MATERIALS NEEDED: Journal/notebook, pen, a handful of dirt, and a trusted tree

PREPARATION: Best done during a new moon cycle with the family and/or during Samhain or Yule.

THE WORK:

1. Have everyone sit around the tree in a circle. Clasp hands and sing, chant, or whisper of sharing knowledge that's come to you through the years.

2. Let the eldest parent step into the circle, take up the dirt, and repeat an incantation of our earthly ties and what we leave behind once they are transferred to another state.

3. Have them regain their seat, take up the paper and pen, write one important piece of wisdom for everyone present, and then hand it to the next eldest.

4. Continue passing the pen and paper until reaching the younger/youngest family members. If they are too young to write, have them draw a picture or scribble. All symbols have meaning.

5. When everyone is finished, stand and hold hands. Dance around the tree together and bow to the Gods.

6. This can be a one-time event but is more potent when repeated annually. As the pages fill, have an elder go through and read some or all the passages, or let individuals absorb them as they wish.

Together No Matter the Weather

(Rite of dedication to each other)

MATERIALS NEEDED: 1 stick to represent every member of the family, 1 candle for each person (whatever color they wish), a garden shovel, a nearby tree, a nice feast

PREPARATION: Have everyone meditate on their stick. They can carve or add whatever decorations they want to it. Scratch the initials of each family member into the side of their specific candle. Set a simple altar with the candles placed at the appropriate positions for the signs. Place the sticks in the center of the altar.

THE WORK:

1. Have everyone stand before the altar at their respective positions. Call the corners to bless your family and ask the Gods to bless this rite.

2. Have everyone pick up their stick and hold it up, then lean them forward to all touch at the ends. Now chant, sing, hum, or whisper of the power of family and sit.

3. Let each person light their candle one by one (young children should have their parent(s) do it for them, and declare their devotion to themselves and their family.

4. When finished, have the eldest person take up the sticks and pile them in the center of the altar.

5. One at a time, from eldest to youngest (young ones being helped or stood in by their parents), Have each person take up their candle and spill wax on the bundle from top to bottom to seal their bonds. Chant, sing, or whisper of sticking together no matter the weather.

6. Call on everyone to blow out their candles and sit together in the stillness for a moment. Then get up and enjoy a lovely feast together.

7. Have a designated person take the sealed bundle of sticks to the tree and bury it while focusing on remaining together no matter what happens.

21

TREE PARENTING
RITUALS

WHETHER PERFORMED DURING A SABBAT OR CAST
ALONE on a weekday, spells that harness the energy of
trees—for the sake of parenting—are potent enough
to climb throughout the life of your child(ren). Some
meet simple needs. Some offer lasting support. Each spell is like its
own world.

When including children in this sacred art, I find it important
to instill a sense of necessity. My kids know that spellwork is to be
performed with careful consideration. It is never to be rushed, and
control is a must. Working to utilize Tree Parenting Spells harbors a
more sensitive nature. These workings must be handled with the care
and context that host the same breed of gentility and strength children
expect from the adults who look after them.

Tilling the Soil of Love

(Strengthening your ability to care for your child(ren)

MATERIALS NEEDED: Salt, water, preferred cleansing herb, brown candle, and matches to light it, small pot/bowl of dirt, 1 stick for each child

PREPARATION: To help focus on what really matters, cast during a waxing moon cycle or on a full moon. Bless the salt and water. Set the altar with the salt to the east, the water to the west, the brown candle at the south, and the dirt to the north, with the sticks and cleansing herb in the center.

THE WORK:

1. Cast a circle with the salt and water. Cleanse the space, then call upon the elements.

2. Kneel before the altar and light the candle. Meditate on it and the electricity that burns within. Think of your ties to your child(ren).

3. Now sit and take the bowl of dirt in your lap. Place your fingertips atop the soil, then press them down. Close your eyes. Dig and turn the earth with your hands, visualizing how we are made from the lands.

4. Take up the stick(s). One-by-one whisper, chant, or sing of the child's individual characteristics and the qualities you best love about them.

5. Lay the stick(s) atop the dirt in the bowl. Close your eyes and meditate on cultivating the personality(ies) that you love, encouraging them, and allowing the best growth for them.

6. Place the bowl back on the altar and walk, sway, or dance around it. Build your energies and celebrate your parental love.

Casting Out Fear to Increase Hope

(Banishing fear to be a good parent)

MATERIALS NEEDED: Salt, water, preferred cleansing herb and matches, dagger, a basket of leaves and twigs, black string and white string, 9 candles to provide light, garden shovel, and a trusted tree.

PREPARATION: Perform on a new or waning moon. Go before a trusted tree and set up a humble altar at the foot of the trunk. Place the salt to the east, water to the west, the dagger to the south, the basket to the north, and the strings in the middle. Set the candles in a circle around this space to provide light.

THE WORK:

1. Light the candles and cleanse the space with cleansing herb whispering, chanting, or singing of casting this spell in the name of the Gods to banish fear in the name of hope.

2. Cast a circle with the salt and water. Call the corners and hold the dagger up to the dark sky drawing on the powers that rise "above as so below."

3. Hold the dagger over the leaves and twigs and let it serve as a conductor of protection and courage. Visualize your concerns and woes for yourself as a parent and your child(ren) or for the parental figure and their child(ren) if performing for someone else.

4. Recite and incantation of driving away fear to find hope and lay the dagger before the leaves and twigs.

5. Take up a leaf and let it represent one of the main concerns. Hold it

up to the sky and express how it affects you/the parent, and your/the child. Then grab a twig and tie it over the leaf, first with some black string and then with white. As you wrap and tie off the string, chant of binding the fear with hope and love. Offering security and, peace, balance.

6. Do this for as many issues as needed.

7. When all are bound, dig a hole between the tree roots and bury the bound fears. Pat the earth and ask the universe to look after your intentions.

8. Bow to the tree and ground yourself.

Spell to Prune Emotional Distress

(To increase personal power when feeling overwhelmed by parenthood)

MATERIALS NEEDED: Salt, water, dagger, small branch with leaves/pine needles still attached, 1 black candle and 1 white candle, matches

PREPARATION: Set an altar with the salt to the east, the water to the west, the candles to the south, the branch to the north, and the dagger in the center.

THE WORK:

1. Cast a circle with the salt and water.

2. Kneel before the candles and chant, sing, or whisper a request for the Gods to aid you in thinning distress from parenting/life and restoring

balance.

3. Stand and take up the dagger. Hold it up and call upon the powers of the elements with their energy "as above," then bring the dagger down to the ground and "so below."

4. Take up the small branch and move the water bowl to the center. Sit before the candles and meditate on the branch. Pour all your frustrations into it. Don't feel guilty for experiencing stress brought on by the pressures that children bring. Let all of it out into the leaves and sticks before you.

5. Now use the dagger to cut away each leaf/pine needle over the water bowl. Speak words of cleansing, purifying yourself and your approach to better handle the issue.

6. Cut away twigs that grow off the main stick. Submerge them too.

7. Now hold the stick up and let your energies flow through it. Focus on the power that is held within at your core.

8. Set the stick before the bowl. Break the circle and ground yourself. Let the candles burn down.

Reaching Understandings

(To resolve family arguments/issues)

MATERIALS NEEDED: 1 candle for each person involved (of the color they choose to represent them, a single stick from a trusted tree, a mirror, and a favorite snack.

PREPARATION: Have everyone meditate on the stick to pour their energies into it. (It can be for 2 people having issues with each other, or more—kids vs. adults, etc.) Set the altar with the candles either next to each other, in a triangle, square, or circle, depending on how many are present. Place the mirror in the center with the stick atop it.

THE WORK:

1. Stand around the altar. Raise arms and breathe deep. Ask the Gods to aid the ability to communicate. Lower your arms and exhale.

2. Call the corners, bringing the power of the elements near.

3. Everyone clasp hands and chant, sing, or whisper of understanding themselves and others to better understand the world around them and their existence.

4. Now have each person light their candle, from oldest to youngest. They must chant, sing, or whisper of their purpose and why they are present.

5. Have the eldest take up the stick, hand it to the youngest, and give them full license to express their feelings openly but respectfully.

6. When they finish, hand them the mirror and instruct them to fully look at themselves, meditate on the meaning in their eyes, and if something is hidden beneath the exterior.

7. Repeat from youngest to eldest. Once everyone has gone, once more, stand together and hold hands. Close eyes and offer any wisdom or resolutions that present themselves. Truly work together to bridge gaps and discuss ways to move forward with love and understanding.

8. Open eyes. Bow to each other and blow out the candles. Go share a snack together and enjoy the company.

Climbing for Clarity

(To seek parenting advice and proper direction)

MATERIALS NEEDED: A trusted tree, black and white ribbons

PREPARATION: Best done alone when feeling lost as a parent. Meditate on each ribbon to charge it with your energy.

THE WORK:

1. Go before a trusted tree. Bow to the boughs. Walk around the trunk 3 times counterclockwise, then turn and walk 3 times clockwise.

2. For those unable or unsure of their climbing abilities, remain on the ground and hand the ribbons as if ascending. For those able, climb up onto the first branch and rest.

3. Breathe deep and pull out a black and white ribbon together. Chant, whisper, or sing of your uncertainty. Ask for guidance on your way along the tree. Tie the black and white ribbon around a small stick or twig growing off the branch.

4. Now climb higher or walk to another section of the tree. Meditate on the unknown aspects of parenting and what is explicitly ailing your mind. Chant, whisper, or sing of the fears, woes, or concerns that come when you feel clouded. Take another pair of black and white ribbons and tie them to the tree.

5. Continue this process, allowing your doubts or lack of direction to be drawn open until you can see through the setbacks and start forming a clearer picture of what truly matters and how to proceed in the future.

6. When the mind has fully opened, and your inner voice feels freed, climb back down/walk back to where you began.

7. Stand before the tree and thank it for offering its wisdom. Bow to the Gods. Then go on your way.

Banishing Decay to Tame Tempers

(To be done during a new moon or waning cycle for moving on from anger and pain caused within the family)

MATERIALS NEEDED: Salt, water, preferred cleansing herb, matches, clippings from a tree (preferably from a spot that was ailing on the plant) placed in a fire-safe bowl, 2 white candles, 1 black candle, and a dagger.

PREPARATION: Set the altar with the salt to the east, water to the west, tree clippings to the north between the 2 white candles, the black candle and dagger to the south, and the fire-safe bowl in the center with the preferred cleansing herb and matches. Best done on a new or waning moon cycle. (If casting for a child, have them sit in front of the black candle.

THE WORK:

1. Cast a circle with salt and water, calling on the power of the elements in the name of the Gods.

2. Light the cleansing herb and cleanse the circle, chanting of balance and purification. Place in a fire-safe bowl to continue burning.

3. Light the white candles, ask the gods to be with you and aid you in banishing your temper or your child's.

4. Hold up the clippings and chant, whisper, or sing of the trouble that we all go through when ailments or frustrations build up, how they cause us to slowly decay from the inside out.

5. Light the black candle and meditate on its flame while touching the

clippings and focusing on the pain/anger inside. Visualize the heat that burns during an outburst and see it as a bright glowing light. Allow yourself or your child to study it and speak to it.

6. Take up the dagger and pierce the clippings at their core. Repeat an incantation of banishing the fires that destroy one from the inside.

7. Now light the clippings in the bowl and focus all your energies on aiding the power of controlled, well-intentioned flames absorbing angry ones, so they lose their rage.

8. Bow your head and relax. Breathe deep and open the circle. Ground yourself/yourselves but leave the candle to burn down.

Protecting Connections

(To keep family bonds strong)

MATERIALS NEEDED: Dagger, quartz crystal or rock found around the home, familiar tree

PREPARATION: This is best done between a parent and child as they age and the roles shift. Teen years, adulthood, etc.

THE WORK:

1. Go before the tree and have the child hold the crystal. Bring the dagger up to the sky and ask the universe to bless your energies "as above," then stab the dagger into the ground and say, "and so below."

2. Sit before the tree with your child and hold hands, covering the crystal/rock together. Meditate on your connection. Think of the bond that was formed from before birth, throughout each stage, all the way to the present.

3. Now visualize the future and your desire to remain close.

4. Chant, sing, or whisper of protecting the familial links that run through you.

5. Take up the dagger and press its blade to the rock as your child holds it steady. Call upon the elements to preserve what is set in "earth, rock, and tree."

6. Gaze up to the branches overhead and bow. Breathe deep. Kiss your child's forehead and have them kiss your cheek. Walk together.

Finding Family in the Trees

(To connect with ancestors and find peace in their influence)

MATERIALS NEEDED: Salt, water, pen paper/crayons or markers, a large green candle

PREPARATION: Works best during a full moon ritual. Place the green candle at the north point of the altar, the salt to the east, the water to the west, and the paper and drawing materials in the center of the triangle this creates. (Can be done solitary or with family and/or friends)

THE WORK:

1. Cast a circle using the salt and calling upon the elements to guide you in the name of the Gods.

2. Light the candle and chant, sing, or whisper of drawing out family ties.

3. Meditate on the candle focusing your energies on your ancestors,

your children, and the people who will come after you.

4. Take up some paper and a pen/crayon/marker. Draw a tree shape. It can be as defined or abstract as you wish. Then close your eyes and visualize your ancestors. Let the power that passed onto you possess your hand/spark creativity.

5. When finished, study your picture, what it means to you, and how you connect to all of existence.

6. Relax and blow out the candle. Open the circle and ground yourself.

Letting go with the Leaves Spell

(To accept the death of a loved one and honor their memory)

MATERIALS NEEDED: Salt, water, preferred cleansing herb, matches, a basket of leaves, picture or memorabilia of a loved one who recently passed on (if it is a child, decorate the alter with as many toys and fond baubles as possible, for older losses just one or two items are all that is needed), 1 large candle to represent the person missing (colored to suit their spirit), 3 white cables and 3 black candles to circle the altar, a potluck feast

PREPARATION: Designed for a group of people but can be done alone. Set the altar with the black and white candles in a circle. Inside, place the salt to the east, water to the west, the leaves to the north, and the candle to honor the person missing at the south. Place the basket of leaves and the items from the loved one in the center.

THE WORK:

1. Cast a circle with salt and water while calling upon the powers of the elements to connect you in the name of the Gods.

2. Light the cleansing herb and cleanse the space. Ignite the black and white circle candles.

3. Then kneel before the altar, light the large candle, and chant, sing, or whisper of the loss and what the person who has passed on meant to you (let everyone present speak if not doing alone).

4. Meditate on the flames. Feel their energy revive you. Let their warmth draw out memories.

5. Now stand and take up the basket of leaves. Let everyone take a small handful. Bow your heads and repeat the incantation of retaining the connection while letting go of the pain of separation so that everyone can move on.

6. Have everyone, from youngest to oldest, hold up a leaf and speak of their favorite memory of the deceased. Keep going around sharing moments until the leaves run out. Scatter them back in the basket and dance around the altar. Allow the power to build, then push it out into the candle, so your connection remains strong.

7. Open the circle and eat, even if you're not hungry. Play favorite songs and videos that spread love and healing. Share photos, hugs, tears, and laughter. Remember to live.

THE MUSIC OF TREES

MUSIC IN THE TREES, MELODIES IN THE FORESTS and natural spaces still uphold cycles in which humanity doesn't always follow. When life becomes too loud, I find myself replenished by these simple vibrations. Summer cicadas serenade my spirit during heat waves. The autumnal crickets slowly soften with each chilly night. Winter winds howl in harmony. Just when I miss the sun, spring storms reawaken the best of nature's musicians.

Our lives are sung through branches and bark. Each season returns differently. New songs are waiting to be sung, but familiarity lingers to offer comfort and love during all the changes of every stage.

I have lived in the heart of a city, spent countless hours in rural towns, and resided in a less-manicured lifestyle of a lower-income suburb where residents aren't held to as many constraints as some intrusive neighborhoods. The trees remain friendly regardless of where I go or who I meet. They offer confidence and an inner rhythm that keeps our deeper instincts connected to the ancient ties that link us to the many generations who came before us.

When in tune with the quaint music of the trees, I can better take care of my physical health, prioritize my mental well-being, and extend the spirit much further than my body can reach. This is mainly because of leaving behind certain modern technologies for hours—if not days—at a time.

There are many benefits to connecting with others faster, but turning off devices and leaving behind background music or television for the purer tones of nature soothes our deeper needs. Instead of subconsciously absorbing frequencies, truly opening oneself to the voices of a forest untainted allows a person to be more mindful. There is a time to relax the mind and a time to sharpen it, and knowing the difference has many benefits, especially when seeking a greater purpose.

Making time for meditations that explore tree music offers heightened power of consciousness. Instead of ignoring bird songs and tree whispers on our way to work or outings, we become more aware of the meaning behind each note, each tiny instrument of life.

Incorporating tree music into ritual is an enlightening experience. Instead of relying on others for compositions that speak to the situation, we become our own conductors. Chants, hums, and even lyrics organically rise from within. This form of personalization solidifies pulsing energies that bind our intentions in an intricate web of possibilities.

When casting spells, tree music encourages a glowing crescendo of understanding and truth. Instead of turning to magic for aid whenever fears arise, the swells of song put us into a state of clarity that better differentiates between want and need.

These different approaches host their own sounds. They can be utilized individually to improve one's habits and lifestyle, but when combined, they also form a rich, full symphony that becomes a lifestyle. I personally prefer both. There are times when simplicity speaks louder than the world of complex efforts.

Single meditations or short rituals aren't just for beginners but for times when the needs of others spill into our schedule. I'm a mother of four. I cannot always skip through the woods talking to pines and oak trees (as much as I want to). There must be time for that, but the occurrences vary.

Properly managing my affairs isn't easy, and things sometimes get into disarray. When the busyness of life drags me down, combined meditations, rituals, and spellwork host the power to push forth changes that suit my needs and reset the nature of my routines (or lack thereof). Every approach can meet success. Our will and the will of the Gods blend through musicality.

22

FINDING TREE
MUSIC

R USTLING LEAVES, RAINDROPS DRIPPING FROM BRANCHES, THE PERCUSSIVE pursuits of woodpeckers drumming on a tree trunk; many natural sounds are hiding beneath the layers of modern machinery and electronics. Anyone can discover the beauty resting in these more subtle tones if attentive enough. Just taking time away from man-made devices opens the senses.

Beyond that, some meditations further explore humanity's friendship with the music of the trees. I love music. I was a born singer and spent decades of my life mastering different styles and performing, but something was always missing. Instead of seeking music as a vocation, I needed to free my spirit from material bonds and let my soul sing in harmony with my spiritual self. Once I recognized my talents as an aspect of being and not some kind of monetary ploy, meditations flourished, and pathways greeted me.

Finding Tree Music

(To better connect with nature)

Step 1: Step outside on a windy day. Close your eyes and breathe deeply.

Step 2: Focus on the rustle of the leaves. Keep your thoughts clear and perceptive to the sounds calling from the trees.

Step 3: Now, become conscious of your heartbeat and how it correlates to the windy song. Sway with the beat. Let it swell and grow.

Step 4: Look to the trees and see how they rock and move with the gales. Trust the sounds and messages that come to you as this dance comes to a close.

Listening to Nature's Instruments

(To increase self-awareness and natural intuition)

Step 1: Take a walk through a forest or wooded area.

Step 2: Clear your mind and breathe deeply. Open your senses and trust the sounds that greet you.

Step 3: Look to the trees and listen to the leaves but focus your ears beyond. Waters, grasses, and more may reveal rushing, whistling, or crunching noises that combine to offer a melodious tune.

Step 4: Walk along to the beat of the natural composition. Allow your heartbeat to synch with this symphony.

Step 5: Now extend your energies and focus on singling out the most prominent sounds. These hold the key to finding answers and understanding personal and natural issues.

Mingling your Voice with the Song of the Trees

(To strengthen your confidence and inner voice)

Step 1: Step outside and sit beneath the most populated area of trees you know of.

Step 2: Close your eyes and stretch your head up as high as possible.

Step 3: Breathe deeply and listen to the sounds of the area. Focus only on natural noises.

Step 4: Now hum along as loud or low as feels comfortable. Let your voice match the tones of the scene.

Step 5: Extend your energies through the power of your voice until you find harmony with nature's song. Let it swell until you become exhausted, then rest and allow the experience to stay with you.

Incorporating Instruments to Increase Understanding

(For heightened intuition)

Step 1: For anyone who plays an instrument and/or doesn't have much mobility, increasing understanding through the music of the trees doesn't have to be done outside. Simply open a window and sit before it on a clear day.

Step 2: Open your mind and listen to the natural sounds drawn into your home: Bird song, leaves shaking, limbs creaking.

Step 3: Bring out your instrument or hum along. Let the vibrations build your energies and extend your powers until you are in a trance.

Step 4: Let the music direct your thoughts. The ideas, images, and sensations that follow will be more vivid and melodic throughout this process.

Step 5: Continue this line of exploration until exhausted. When finished, sit back and relax.

Focusing through Forest Sounds

(To your better focus and appreciate living in the present)

Step 1: When unable to sort through thoughts or emotions, take a trip to a friendly forest and find a comfortable spot to sit on a bench or in a public field/clearing or picnic area.

Step 2: Place your hands at your sides flat down and sit tall. Breathe deep.

Step 3: Close off all your senses, then focus on just hearing. Place all your emphasis on the power of sound and truly listen without interruption.

Step 4: As you bond with the natural song, recall a favorite sound and think of it as well-defined as possible, so much so that you can hear it perfectly replicated. Repeat it with the current tones. Let them mingle.

Step 5: Remain focused on the sound. Hold onto its exact notation for as long as possible. Then when your ears ring or your head begins to throb, relax and let it go.

Step 6: Repeat as often as needed.

Percussive Purposes

(To connect with your greater purpose)

Step 1: Take a walk and find a suitable stick or a couple of rocks.

Step 2: Go before the nearest tree to your home or sit with a potted plant if unable. Set the stick or rocks before you and close your eyes. Breathe deep and hold your hands over the item(s).

Step 3: Focus your senses on hearing. Close everything else off as best as possible.

Step 4: Allow the natural rhythm and vibrations to captivate you. Revel in their excellent work.

Step 5: When ready, take up the stick or one of the rocks. Click the rocks together or beat the stick on the tree to join in with this ancient song.

Step 6: Stop and start as needed. Allow your energies to grow during this process. As you contribute your beat, form a clear picture of yourself as if watching from beyond. How do you sit? Why are you there? Question the greater meaning and enjoy the answers that greet you.

Embracing Calming Tones

(To reduce stress and find peace)

Step 1: To better cope with the hectic nature of life, open a window near a tree by your home or go out and sit at the foot of a nearby tree.

Step 2: Close your eyes and let the rhythm of the sounds take over. Breathe in and out with them. Slow and easy.

Step 3: Recall what's been stressing you. Let it surface as you continue to focus and breathe with nature

Step 4: Imagine the tree's song coaxing your stress from your body. Its melodies can offer solutions. Harmony is possible through a gentle partnership with nature's voice.

Step 5: Once fully relaxed, think of the song and remember it.

Answers in the Wind

(To heighten intuition and your connection to nature)

Step 1: On a windy day, go outside to a favorite tree or open a window and listen to the rushing leaves.

Step 2: It takes skill to decipher the many messages transmitted in these gusts. Clear your mind and focus on reaching out. Forget your specific issues and expand your power, humming in tune with the wind as it howls and drifts through your space.

Step 3: Every sound has a purpose. Focus on them one at a time.

Step 4: Let the music take over and send you drifting into a trance-like state.

Step 5: Ask the trees to reveal their secrets to you. Close your eyes and rely only on sound.

Step 6: Be perceptive. Be ready.

Step 7: When unable to continue, bow to the tree and thank the Gods.

Voices of the Gods/Universe

(To speak with the Gods and better understand them)

Step 1: On a clear night, open the windows or go out and stand beside a favorite tree. Place hands on the windowsill or the tree, palms down.

Step 2: Breathe deep and look to the sky. Pool your energies and feel the heat within growing and encourage it to spread.

Step 3: Listen to the night calls and let yourself fall into their trance. Hum or sing along as needed.

Step 4: Close your eyes and feel the night air gliding by. Listen and be attentive to your purpose. Focus on your individual role as a voice in the choir, an instrument of life. Let that connection draw forth a stronger bond between yourself and the earth. Sing along with it as you feel compelled to do. Humming externally or internally does not matter so long as you reach beyond yourself.

Step 5: Visualize your contribution combining with the notes to make a great song that reaches across the world and stretches through the universe.

Step 6: As you envision this great work, open yourself up to speaking with the universe. Talk to the divine out loud, in song, or internally. Give it time. Responses may take time but will have a lasting impact.

Step 7: Once exhausted, rest and reflect.

23

TREE MUSIC
RITUALS

I T DOESN'T TAKE A MUSICIAN TO INCORPORATE NATURAL music
into ritual. Reaching out to wild spaces and drawing out the sounds
of trees and the creatures within them is something anyone can
do. Whether a music lover, instrumentalist, or tone-deaf karaoke
fan, the trees don't discriminate.

There is understanding in the cries of a forest. Pain and triumph,
anger and fear. Strong feelings pull forth our most honest emotions
and aid us in our workings. Finding my personal beat to celebrate
an occasion puts me in sync with reality while allowing me to better
connect to my spirituality.

The Opening Number

(Ritual to introduce or increase natural music into spiritual practices)

MATERIALS NEEDED: A single white candle or a fire pit, matches or flint rocks, bell, instrument or voice, and water or wine

PREPARATION: If doing this indoors, open windows and place the candle in the center of the altar with the bell at the east side, the water/wine to the west, and the instrument or self to the south facing north. If doing outdoors with a fire pit, build up the fire with proper kindling, sticks, and or logs, and stand a safe distance back with the bell to your right and the water/wine to the left (If using an instrument, place it carefully at your feet). Best done on a new or waxing moon.

THE WORK:

1. Stand before the ritual space and breathe deeply. Close your eyes and clear your mind.

2. Focus on the sounds swirling around you. Is there whistling wind, trees creaking, animals stirring, or a calm stillness that offers the space of silence? Let the energy of the area inspire you.

3. Now light the candle or fire and stare at the flame(s). Watch the fire dance and listen to its hiss, the tones of its pop or crackle. Extend your energies with the aid of the light's warmth.

4. When ready, bring up the bell and ring it 3-times as fast or slow as compelled to. Then listen. Be conscious of your heartbeat and the rhythm of the noises mingling with you and your ritual.

5. Ring the bell 3 more times, then take a sip of water or wine. Set the bell down and take up your instrument or raise your voice in song.

Hum or create your own lyrics to match the beat of your body, the fire, and the natural setting.

6. Allow this song to grow. Forget time and enjoy the moments. Allow your heart to swell and reverberate with every pitch. Find divinity in primitive song and appreciate whatever signals or messages come through it.

7. Continue until exhausted. When finished, allow the fire to die out and ground yourself by placing bare feet on the ground while spreading out the ashes and watching the flames lower.

Wilding Your Inner Song

(To find deeper comfort with your spiritual ties)

MATERIALS NEEDED: Wind chimes, 2 sticks, and a wooden cup or bowl of water

PREPARATION: Take a walk or go outside and find 2 matching sticks. Meditate on your spirit and its connection to the wild world. Place the bowl or cup of water at the center of your altar or beneath a friendly tree. Set 1 stick on either side and place the chimes between yourself and the bowl at the center. .

THE WORK:

1. Hold the chimes over the bowl and let them set the tone for this ritual. If there is no wind or they do not chime, gently shake them to induce the intended song.

2. Breathe deep and hum in tune with the chimes. Now glance around. See how your song matches the movements and actions of the natural

surroundings. If indoors, look out the windows. Open the senses and become wholly aware.

3. Take up the sticks and drum along the rim of the water bowl or cup. Watch how the ripples on the liquid surface match this song. Think of the din of the chimes and continue to hum. Close your eyes and feel the pulse of life running through the entire area.

4. Let your energies build. Open your eyes, stand, sing and/or dance around the space as if you were a bird free to fly.

5. When reaching the height of your efforts, stop, draw your arms down but tilted out from your sides, and stare up into the sky. Welcome the sight of birds or just trees reaching high above. Extend your energies and feel the elevation as you finish this display.

6. Sit and contemplate your role as a creature of this great work and how your contribution is linked to all other beings.

Drawing Out Tree Lyrics

(To increase energy)

MATERIALS NEEDED: Wand, handmade crown/head-wreath, familiar tree

PREPARATION: Take a nature walk and collect materials to create a head wreath. Bless it with your energies through meditation and wear it for the ritual. If the wand still needs to be blessed or charmed, do so as well.

THE WORK:

1. Wear your wreath and go before the tree. Stand facing the sun (for

bolder answers in pure light) or the moon (for softer realizations drawn from the enchanting glow).

2. Point your wand at the tree and chant to find the words for your song, the words that connect you best to all beings and offer strength when feeling weak.

3. Now walk around the tree. Hear the music linking you to the great plant. Hum or sing along as you go around at the pace best suited for this intimate connection.

4. Turn and go around in the opposite direction. Let the lyrics breathe.

5. When lightheaded or at the peak of your energy, face the sun or moon once more. Point your wand at it in the sky and draw the tip from the horizon to the tree, thanking the Gods for the voice within.

6. Bow and lay down/ground yourself.

Understanding Forest Melodies

(A nature divination for heightened intuition)

MATERIALS NEEDED: A metal bowl of water or wine, a single stick, a handful of leaves or grass, 3 rocks of different sizes, flower buds or fully blooming flowers, a fairy ring of trees in a forest or wooded area (if this is not possible it can be done before a few potted plants) PREPARATION: Bless the liquid for your purpose by meditating on it. Set the bowl in the center of the fairy tree ring. Place the other items around it in a circle within the ring.

THE WORK:

1. Sit before the bowl and the items surrounding it in the ring.

2. Close your eyes and breathe deeply. Open your senses. Be aware of the sounds filling the space.

3. Take your prominent pointer finger and drag it along the bowl's surface at a steady pace.

4. Continue this and pick up your stick. Drop the stick in as you continuously drag your fingertip over the edge of the bowl. Listen to the splash and watch the ripples.

5. Pick up the handful of leaves or grass. Drop them in the water slowly. Feel the impact, the transfer of energy, and the slight pianissimo addition to this "song."

6. Now chant, sing, or whisper a request for the forest to sing to you like a beast.

7. Take up the smallest rock and drop it in, all the while still moving the finger over the rim of the bowl. Focus on the sound and the ripples that follow.

8. Repeat with the next smallest rock, then the biggest.

9. Last, sprinkle the flowers/buds into this symphony. Truly listen and be open to your observations.

10. Close your eyes and meditate on hearing all the forest can say.

11. When exhausted, stand before the bowl. Bow before the trees, offering them the contents by spilling the liquid in the circle.

12. Take a walk and ground yourself.

Truth in Tree Song

(To strengthen your connection with trees and nature)

MATERIALS NEEDED: 2 sticks, a pair of finger symbols, a pair of bells, trusted tree (indoor or outdoor)

PREPARATION: Find a pair of similar-looking sticks or pick up a pair of drumsticks. Best done with 3 people but can be expanded or solitary.

THE WORK:

1. Stand before the tree and raise your arms to the sky. Breathe in and extend your energies.

2. Walk around the tree and hum, chant, or whisper focusing on asking to find the truth.

3. Now hit the sticks against each other, clang the symbols, and ring the bells as you pick up the pace circling the tree. (Do it together or 1 at a time—let the atmosphere decide).

4. When the power of this rite is felt strongly, turn to the tree and drum on it, press the symbols to it, and ring the bells on it one at a time. (If in a group, have the others continue circling and singing/humming. If alone, return to circling after each instrument is used.)

5. Let your ears ring. Tune in to that frequency and truly listen. Absorb the energy.

6. Once exhausted, stop and sit before the tree. If it is large enough, sit with your back pressed to the trunk and face out. Close your eyes and be open to the answers that come.

7. When finished, bow to the tree, thank the gods, and lay down and ground yourself.

Enhancing Emotional Connections

(To strengthen self-control)

MATERIALS NEEDED: A long black or white ribbon, a wooded area or indoor plant, a dagger

PREPARATION: less the ribbon with emotional energies. Let all your hidden joys, fears, memories, hopes, and more out. Carry the dagger in a holster or place it in an area where you will end the journey.

THE WORK:

1. Hold the ribbon in your hands and take a walk in the woods or sit before a houseplant if unable.

2. With each step/moment, recall past issues where you lost control of your emotions.

3. After walking to a friendly tree/or enough time, hold the ribbon up to the great plant. Chant, sing, or whisper of allowing yourself to love others and be there for the world and yourself.

4. Unsheathe the dagger and wrap the ribbon around its blade slowly, covering every hint of it.

5. Hold the dagger up to the sky, then point the tip at the tree. Pool your energies and stab the blade into the dirt, releasing all misgivings. Let the tree absorb your fears and draw courage from the roots.

6. Leave the dagger on the ground and step back. Bow to the tree. Look to the gods and remind yourself that it is okay to feel however you need to in any situation as long as you always trust yourself.

7. Pull the dagger from the ground. Sit and meditate on being open and connected without allowing naivety.

Discovering Your Personal Beat

(To be done during Sabbat celebration for increased intuition)

MATERIALS NEEDED: Walking stick
PREPARATION: Best done around or on a Sabbat.

THE WORK:

1. Take a walk on a forest path. Breathe deep. Open your senses. Observe nature's beauty.

2. Focus on your surroundings and look for a fair-sized walking stick. When discovered, stop for a moment. Hold it up to the trees and close your eyes. Build your energies and send them into the stick.

3. Now walk with the stick. Feel your body move in time. Tap the end of the walking stick in rhythm while clearing your mind and relying on deeper instincts.

4. Be perceptive to the thoughts and images that come to mind. Let them lead you on this journey.

5. When exhausted, sit and relax. Ground yourself upon the earth.

Synchronizing Magic Melodies

(To follow your greater purpose)

MATERIALS NEEDED: Small hand mirror or compact, wooded area

PREPARATION: Bless the mirror with your energies to better recognize synchronicity.

THE WORK:

1. Take a walk in the woods, holding the mirror down.

2. Breathe deep. Open your senses and let your inner power grow with each step.

3. When perfectly at ease, hold the mirror before your face and look yourself in the eye. Chant words of connection and finding the patterns that bind all our lives. Repeat the words 3-times.

4. Now turn and walk back the way you came but with the mirror facing upwards. Be aware of the timing. Hear the spirit of the trees as they repeat certain movements.

5. Listen to the melody of your surroundings and mingle your energies with it. You may find a sense of recognition, déjà vu, or other instances that entangle themselves into your spiritual consciousness.

6. At the end of your walk, look back to where you came from and bow. Thank the universe for preserving certain elements of life, and use what you learned.

Harmonies to Reach the gods

(To connect with the gods through music)

MATERIALS NEEDED: Guitar, violin, or another acoustic string instrument (all skill levels are adequate) and a favorite tree

PREPARATION: Meditate on your instrument and bless it with your energies.

THE WORK:

1. Sit before the tree and hold your instrument in your lap.

2. Close your eyes and breathe deeply. Visualize the tree's energy and extend yours to it.

3. Now take up the instrument and begin to play something new. Let the melody be as easy or difficult as needed. Don't worry about mistakes. Sharps and flats are part of life. Just keep playing. Keep the music flowing.

4. Begin humming along. Rock and/or sway with this improvised tone.

5. Let go of all reservations. Open the senses and sing to the tree, to yourself, and to the gods. Repeat words of seeking purpose, wisdom, and fulfillment. Sing of gratitude, love, and understanding. Sing from experience but focus on the joys you seek. Let the song weave itself. Don't force it.

6. Harmonize for as long as you deem necessary. When exhausted, end playing and welcome silence.

7. Look to the tree and up above. Breathe in the atmosphere. Trust your inner voice and any new ideas that may present themselves.

8. Look to the tree and ground yourself.

24

TREE MUSIC
SPELLS

RAFTING A SONG IS A SPELL IN ITSELF. The words twist out and wrap around you with the power to captivate others and draw forth like-minded individuals. Tree music in spellwork hosts the same kind of energy. It is eternal, timeless, and incredibly intimate.

Protections, animal bonding, and other specific linking spells are best solidified with certain sounds or rhythms. When working with familiars, they craft special bonds. Song and dance is an expression that exudes the best of our animalistic tendencies. When giving in to the harmonies of tree music, I find small animals drawn to my outdoor practices and feel myself more highly linked to them and the land. The spells that evolve from this are unlike the others I have known.

Spell to Call Your Guides

(To find direction in life)

MATERIALS NEEDED: Sticks (enough for you to comfortably kneel in), water, salt, preferred cleansing herb, lapis lazuli rock

PREPARATION: Gather sticks. Best done on the full moon.

THE WORK:

1. Place the sticks in a circle around your workspace but set 2 in the workspace. Set the water to the west, the salt to the east, the preferred cleansing herb to the south, and the stone at the north.

2. Consecrate the circle with the salt and water, then cleanse the space with the preferred cleansing herb.

3. Now kneel at the center of the circle. Clear your mind and take up the lapis lazuli. Close your eyes and hold it to your forehead between your eyes. Sing, chant, or whisper asking for guidance.

4. Now place the stone before you and take up your pair of sticks. Beat them on the ground on either side of the stone. Drum out a steady rhythm and keep chanting/singing. Let the music draw energy from the stone. Extend your spirit with each beat.

5. Let the music take hold for as long as needed.

6. When exhausted, lay down holding the stone in your prominent hand and the sticks in the other. Listen to yourself and your surroundings.

7. Trust what you know and break the circle. Then ground yourself.

Extending Tree Music to Connect with Others

(To welcome new friendships/connections)

MATERIALS NEEDED: Pair of sticks, a friendly tree, wind chimes (as many as desired), salt, water, preferred cleansing herb, a white or black candle, and matches

PREPARATION: Bless the chimes with your desire to connect with others. Charge the sticks with your personal power.

THE WORK:

1. Take items before the tree. Place the candle in the center with the sticks on either side. Set the water to the west, the salt to the east, the preferred cleansing herb and matches at the south, and the wind chimes to the north of the candle.

2. Cast a circle using the salt and water, then cleanse the space with the preferred cleansing herb.

3. Clear your mind and stand before the tree. Look to it and hum or sing of connecting with others as the tree's roots reach out below you.

4. Bend down and light the ritual candle.

5. Take up the sticks and beat them around the candle, continuing this song.

6. When your energies are built up, set the sticks down and grasp a set of chimes. Hang them in the tree. Let their music drift and extend your spirit.

7. Repeat this process as many times as possible, humming/singing, then beating the sticks and hanging a set of chimes.

8. Then step back and listen. Bow to the tree. Look to the universe

stretching above and be thankful.

9. Walk with purpose and go ground yourself.

Motivating Through Nature's Song

(To be done during the waxing moon cycle for enhanced personal power and motivation)

MATERIALS NEEDED: Salt, water, preferred cleansing herb, citrine stone, trusted tree

PREPARATION: Best done during the waxing moon cycle.

THE WORK:

1. Set the stone at the foot of the tree.

2. Cast a circle with the salt and water, then cleanse it with a cleansing herb.

3. Kneel before the stone and meditate on its energies. Feel its energetic light surround you as you listen to the sounds of nature.

4. Look up to the tree branches and stand. Chant or sing of finding motivation as you circle the tree and clap in time. Expel your energies and dance within the circle, allowing the power of the citrine and the tree to rejuvenate you.

5. At the height of your song, stop and kneel once more. Absorb the atmosphere. Let it wash over you and flow through your body.

6. Now lay down and close your eyes. Focus on the music of the tree. Ground yourself in your purpose.

7. When ready, sit up and bow to the tree. Thank the Gods for such an experience.

Protection Song Spell

(To protect yourself and natural spaces)

MATERIALS NEEDED: A handful of dirt, a small cup of water, a black or white candle, matches, and a tree or wooded area

PREPARATION: Bless the water. This can be done at any time. Saliva can be used in immediate danger, and burning a stick will suffice.

THE WORK:

1. Scatter the dirt in a circle around you before a tree or inside a wooded area.

2. Walk along the circle, staying on the inside, and flick water over the dirt to consecrate it.

3. Place the candle in the center and kneel before it. Clear your mind and open your senses.

4. Start your song by humming. Focus on the protective energies within yourself, the circle, and the tree or woods. Let your song come to life as the power increases. Sing of safety from harm.

5. Raise your voice as loud as can be. Let it fill you and your circle until you fear nothing.

6. When exhausted, remain inside the circle for as long as necessary, but ground yourself and trust in the universe when breaking it.

Finding Familiars

(*To attract animal companions*)

MATERIALS NEEDED: Bowl of dirt, a small cup of water, a natural space where wildlife frequents. (If seeking a specific animal, a memento of that type. Ex: a feather for a bird, a clump of hair for a mammal, etc.)

PREPARATION: Bless the water. (If using a memento, charge it with your personal energies.)

THE WORK:

1. Go to the natural space and create a circle with the bowl of dirt.

2. Consecrate the space with the water and sit in the center of this ring. (Hold the memento if obtained)

3. Breathe deep and open your senses. Feel your inner animal clawing to break free. Let that energy build until it can no longer remain caged inside.

4. Release that power into the circle and close your eyes. Feel the warmth surrounding you. Push it out into the surrounding area. Call to the animals with your spirit.

5. Be patient. Nature moves at its own pace. Nothing can be rushed in the wild world.

6. When spotting a familiar, simply observe and extend your energies. Let them observe you and respond.

7. If no encounter occurs, don't be discouraged. This can be attempted as many times as desired.

8. When you are alone again, break the circle and bow to the trees. Look to the universe and be thankful.

Building Bonds

(To strengthen the connection to others and your purpose)

MATERIALS NEEDED: Salt, water, preferred cleansing herb and matches, jade stone, small drum, and trusted tree

PREPARATION: Bless the water. Charge the stone with your energies.

THE WORK:

1. Go before the tree and set the stone at the foot of it at the northernmost point. Place the salt to the east, the water to the west, the cleansing herb and matches to the south, and the drum in the center.

2. Cast a circle with the salt and water, then cleanse it by burning the cleansing herb.

3. Now sit before the drum. Reach over it and place one hand on the stone, the other on the drum. Chant or sing of leading with love to build unbreakable bonds with the world around you.

4. Look up to the branches above. Listen to them. Now take up the drum and let your heartbeat out.

5. Open yourself to the song. Sing or hum along, focusing on words or the desire to reach out.

6. If accompanied by others, take turns drumming, get up, and dance between playing. If alone, get up, dance with the beat in your memory, and keep singing.

7. When the energies are at their peak, kneel before the stone and hold it in your hands. Close your eyes. Visualize your purpose turned

into reality.

8. Then set the stone down and stand once more. Place hands on the tree's trunk and ground yourself, then break the circle.

Casting Greater Links to the land (and its history)

(To connect with specific spaces and their past)

MATERIALS NEEDED: Salt, water, preferred cleansing herb and matches, flower seeds (to be planted around a favorite tree), and garden shovel.

PREPARATION: Bless the water.

THE WORK:

1. Cast a circle with the salt and water, then cleanse the space with a cleansing herb.

2. Now meditate on the seeds. Extend your energies to them and their potential life. Visualize the roots taking hold and linking themselves to the land, getting to know the tree.

3. Now stand and place your hands on the tree trunk. Close your eyes and envision the tree's reach, above and below. See how it extends and looks over and through the land and holds the potential to do so for many ages.

4. Now take up the shovel and hum. Let the sound grow into a song. Plant the seeds around the tree and sing of planting your link to the land. Let your intent pass from you to the seeds.

5. When finished, pat the ground, and thank the Gods. Then ground

yourself and break the circle.

6. Return to the area as often as possible. Sing to the flowers and let them sing to you.

Increasing Your Personal Evolution

(To accept change and embrace personal growth)

MATERIALS NEEDED: Salt, water, preferred cleansing herb and matches, singing bowl, white jade stone, a white or black candle, and a wooded area or friendly tree

PREPARATION: Bless the water. Charge the stone with your energy.

THE WORK:

1. Set the candle at the center of a comfortable area in the woods or before a friendly tree. Place the salt to the east, the water to the west, the cleansing herb and matches to the south, and the singing bowl to the north with the white jade inside.

2. Cast a circle with the salt and water, then clear the space by burning the cleansing herb.

3. Pick up the stone and walk along the inner boundaries of the circle. Hum and let your spirit free a song. Sing words that feel right.

4. Then go before the candle and sing of evolving beyond your current form. Kneel and light it.

5. Take the singing bowl into your lap and sit back. Set the stone in its place. Now let the bowl accompany you in your song/melody of

enlightenment. Trust yourself and the spell. Ask the Gods to help guide you as you follow your purpose.

6. When at the height of the song, freeze and focus on the power pulsing around. Absorb and embrace it.

7. Then bow to the tree(s) and ground yourself.

Tuning Beyond

(To connect with the gods and the dead)

MATERIALS NEEDED: Salt, water, preferred cleansing herb and matches, 2 singing bowls, 2 amethyst stones, a black or white candle, and a secluded forest area or trusted tree

PREPARATION: Bless the water. Charge the stone with your energy.

THE WORK:

1. Walk to your space and set the candle in the center of the workspace. Preferably with your back to a friendly tree. Set the salt to the east, water to the west, cleansing herb and matches to the south, and the singing bowls to the north with the stones (one in each bowl).

2. Cast a circle with the salt and water, then cleanse the space by burning the cleansing herb.

3. Stand and raise your arms up to the trees above. Then reach down and light the candle. Sing of the Gods and those that came before you. Focus on opening yourself to powers beyond this life.

4. Pick up the stones, one in each hand. Lean against the tree or as close as possible and visualize the vast expanse of existence. Feel the

amethyst's power and let it aid you on this journey—sing of it.

5. Set the stones back in the singing bowls and go sit before them. Play these beautiful instruments. Let their tones inspire you to let go of earthly time.

6. Sing along with these melodies utilizing lyrics that call to specific Gods, ancestors, loved ones, or energies you wish to communicate with. Let the music do the rest.

7. Trust what you hear, see, and feel. Be open but remain aware. When exhausted, meditate on what you've experienced. Then break the circle and ground yourself.

AGING LIKE THE TREES

YOUTH IS FOR THE INEXPERIENCED. IT HAS ITS place in our life, but we eventually grow out of mainstream beauty concepts and discover the stunning nature of embracing our bodies as they are. When comparing a sapling to great Redwoods, there is much to learn.

The young hold much potential. There is hope and change within their existence. These are all essential elements of life, but the age-old wisdom of experience must also be accepted. Balance is not just found in utilizing the magic of trees to guide us when change comes, but gradually, as we age and take on the roles our parents and grandparents left behind.

Like the sequoias and pin oaks, like cacti and seaweed, humanity too can age with grace and beauty. The trees are perfect examples for us to embrace our creases and wrinkles as signs of wisdom. Within each mark or scar lives a story. Fading hair and laugh lines have a lot to say. A rough exterior can host decay, while the most flexible trunks exude health and vitality.

I personally look forward to my elderly years. If I am fortunate enough to reach them, I wish to spread my love of life to younger generations. Nothing is stopping me from doing that now, and I do at times, but there is a certain expectation and image of myself that I long to reach in my later years. It is a simple enough task linked to my childhood when my grandparent's neighbor doted on my sister, my cousins, and me. It is connected to my experiences going to nursing homes and singing for the residents who weren't just my relatives. It is linked to a reverence for those who came before me.

Some of these influences embraced their fate. They aged with strong wisdom, like the trees. I, too, wish to age like the trees. I want to keep learning and reaching until I am tall enough to pass on a wealth of knowledge. Now in the middle of my life, there is plenty of room to help others grow. Even in childhood, we have some insights to share with others, but the urgency makes for stronger energy at the end of one's life.

That energy builds through time. Memories and lessons build up. If one is dedicated, they can create a positive circle around them that aids others in creating similar circles, and thus the pattern continues and spreads until the entire forest is lifted.

There are timeless influences across the globe. The shelter of the trees and their resourceful grains, the plants that scatter across plains, underwater reefs, and desert cacti; all these living ties to the land host the same energy. That energy can be utilized to find joy in meeting new years with excitement. Instead of fearing death, or the years leading up to it, we can take courage. That power lives within ourselves and the trees that speak to us.

Meditations to welcome laugh lines, wrinkles, and skin spots draw from this power. They elevate one's perception of themselves without overinflating their sense of worth. When one accepts their fate and embraces it, they can laugh easier and smile more. Our eyes shine beyond our years when we do not hide from the inevitable.

From that mentality, rituals spark. Rituals to welcome each year, to better understand new limits, and to discover new talents host a continued spark of energy that is sometimes daunted by reality.

The rituals and habits we take with us on the journey into antiquity may require aid. At times the need calls for heightened intuition, strength, or patience. Spells are not just for the young. They provide the variety in life that elderly spiritualists must look to. These practices can make the golden years of our lives genuinely shine. Nothing is brighter than someone who loves who they are throughout every role of their life.

25

TREE AGING
MEDITATIONS

COMING TO TERMS WITH MORTALITY ISN'T EASY. WE all experience life's stages in different ways, but looking to the trees when needing guidance, reassurance, or even just a sense of self aids the process of acceptance and under-standing. By root, bark, limb, and leaf, trees display aspects that honor aging. Meditating on this lends peace despite the unknown.

Grounding Expectations

(To accept the beauty of aging)

Step 1: Sit beneath a tree and place your hands on the ground, preferably where the roots are unearthed a bit.

Step 2: Close your eyes and breathe deeply. Clear your mind.

Step 3: Now focus on the roots beneath you. Think of their meaning and power, how they are not often seen or known as the most beautiful part of the tree, but without them, this being could not exist. Let that idea consume you.

Step 4: Think of yourself and your life. Which aspects are most important? What has nourished you beneath the surface? Follow the thoughts that surface with this idea.

Step 5: Merge the two. See yourself as the tree. Root yourself in the grounding of life. Visualize everything you are and embrace the true nature of budding into old age.

Step 6: When exhausted, sit back, and open your eyes. Look to the sky and rub your hands together. Bow to the tree and take what you've learned.

Tending Broken Branches

(To ease aches and pains of aging)

Step 1: Sit, stand, or lay down wherever you feel most comfortable.

Step 2: Extend your arms overhead and gently stretch. Breathe deep and relax.

Step 3: Reach down as far as possible and feel your body release tension. Breathe deep, then relax.

Step 4: Now gaze above you. Let your eyes relax and focus on what ails you. We often spend so much time trying not to think about the pain that we forget to tend to it when we have the ability.

Step 5: Place a hand over the hurting area (if mental pain, place a hand on the forehead, if spiritual, put a hand over the heart). Now recall a time when you were young. When you ran freely and were as limber as the youngest sapling. Feel that energy and stretch your body as needed. Be calm and take your time. Do not force anything.

Step 6: Now visualize the biggest tree you've ever seen. Think of its great strength and how it rocks and sways through life. Rock and sway like the tree, as exaggerated or small as needed.

Step 7: Think of your age as a gift. Now is the time to truly care for yourself. You have no other choice now. This is when you must cater to yourself, your body's needs, and your being as much as possible.

Step 8: Relax and meditate on who you are and what you love about life. No matter how simple or small, there is always at least one thing to aid your mental and spiritual state as well as your body.

Step 9: When unable to focus any longer, clear your mind and breathe easily.

Growing with Grace

(To appreciate your life journey)

Step 1: Sit before a trusted tree or a friendly potted plant. Put your chin to your chest and close your eyes. Visualize yourself as you were in childhood.

Step 2: Breathe deep and sit tall. Now, remember your early adulthood years. Think of what you wished to accomplish and what you enjoyed in those days.

Step 3: Reach your arms above your head or as much as you can comfortably to stretch. Take your time with each step. Do not rush yourself. Enjoy the meditation. Visualize yourself growing into middle age and how you branched out.

Step 4: Now stand and look up. (If unable, hold your head high and just look up). See yourself as you are now. Smile on the life you have been allowed to live and think of what still brings you joy. What foods, drinks, games, and aspects of life remain enjoyable? Who are the people you love and look forward to seeing?

Step 5: Remember an elderly person you admired as a child. Why did you care for them? What made them so important to you that you still remember their legacy? Revel in the memories.

Step 6: Breathe deep and focus on how you can embody the beauty this person brought into your life and how you can share it with a young person and pass that energy on.

Rooting yourself in the Spiritual

(To increase focus on your spiritual self above your physical body)

Step 1: Sit outside on a nice day. Breathe deep and clear your mind.
Step 2: Look to the trees or other vegetation before you. Think of

each one as a friend, a being that breathes and lives just like each person you meet.

Step 3: Let your consciousness draw forth the inner connection to the trees. Feel each breath and its origin, how your lives are intertwined.

Step 4: Now look to the sky. Feel the sunshine nourish your skin.

Step 5: Find a leaf to focus on. Turn your attention towards it and imagine the great energy that comes from drawing in the sun's rays and converting that power into nourishment for the entire plant.

Step 6: Gaze up into the sky once more. Close your eyes. Truly feel the rays of the sun. Draw them in. Ask them to nourish and sustain you.

Step 7: Now, think of the earth and all its creatures. Feel that tug, that binding knowledge that connects you more deeply. Expand it beyond. Journey through the sensations of exploring the links we all have to our surroundings, not just the immediate setting but the universe as a whole.

Step 8: Let your heart swell. Push all fears aside and listen for messages hiding there for you.

The BIG Questions

(To increase spiritual knowledge and wisdom)

Step 1: Sit before a tree or a picture of a tree. Study each limb. See how the branches move together yet in different directions all at once.

Step 2: Think of each branch as a question seeking an answer and the space around them, the pool of wisdom opening up as time goes by.

Step 3: Look to the bottom branches. The simple questions lie there.

Close your eyes and let your simple questions surface. Whether personal or broader, meditate on the little things that have followed you lately.

Step 4: Extend your energies and call to the answers which float around you.

Step 5: Now rest for a minute. Clear your mind and smile at this exercise.

Step 6: Look to the middle branches. The median questions lie there. Close your eyes and once more allow yourself to ask all the questions that are more difficult but not unanswerable. Meditate on the more eminent things, the concerns which have grown over time.

Step 7: Extend your energies and call to the answers, which may take more work to accept. Prepare yourself and be understanding.

Step 8: Last, look to the tallest branches. They may be more worn and broken in places, but they hold the most difficult questions and seek the truest answers of life. Like those great limbs, close your eyes and ponder the scariest questions. Unlock that part of yourself that isn't afraid to look into the truly unknown and the potential that is hidden in it.

Step 9: Extend your energies. Call to the answers with all your power. Explore everything you know and more. Let your spirit go beyond the depths of your mind and blossom with the answers of life.

Step 10: Relax and ground yourself. Drink tea or water and be content.

Loving Life

(To enhance appreciation and enjoyment)

Step 1: Sit outside or by a window and look to the trees.

Step 2: Breathe deep and clear your mind.

Step 3: Now gaze at the life before you. From root to trunk, branches, and trees, gaze at the greenery. Smile at how it has persevered through storms and human development.

Step 4: Focus on the animals that rely on the trees. Watch their little dance. See the birds and other creatures going about their daily business as if nothing will ever change.

Step 5: Think of how our little routines and rituals make each day special. Recall your favorite part of each day and what it means to you. Meditate on the energy you derive from that simple comfort.

Step 6: When unable to focus, wave to the animals and the trees. Smile on yourself and your own dance of life.

Honoring the Elder Within

(To build personal power through respect for the elder you are becoming)

Step 1: Sit before a tree or window. Look outside and think back.

Step 2: See how big everything and everyone was when you were younger. How tall and strong your elders seemed.

Step 3: Every sapling has its elder. And as it grows, it too, must learn when to be flexible and when to stand firm. Now that you have weathered the seasons of life, sit tall.

Step 4: Think of yourself as the grand elder tree.

Step 5: Trust in your ability to draw from your experiences.

Step 6: Remember how you have succeeded in times of struggle.

Step 7: Recall how you had to compromise under certain circumstances and stand tall in others.

Step 8: Breathe deep and take on the crown of elder wisdom. Don't be afraid to offer advice when it is asked. Trust in the answers that age has provided you, and gently offer them to those willing to sit in your shade.

Reaching for the Gods

(Strengthening your connection with the Gods)

Step 1: First thing on a cold winter morning, sit up and breathe in the chilly air.

Step 2: Look to the light. Think of how it sustains you and the trees that surround the globe.

Step 3: Close your eyes. Visualize the warmth pulsing through you and every other living being.

Step 4: See the sun in all his glory. Burning brilliant and illuminating existence.

Step 5: Think of the moon and her soft role in comforting and watching over us even when she does not shine during the daytime.

Step 6: Now focus your energy on reaching out to the universe and the power of existence. Let your spirit vibrate. Let your being emanate with life and love.

Step 7: Reach up and stretch your body. Let your spine tingle. Feel everything and walk with purpose.

Finding Shade

(To find balance in aging)

Step 1: Before bed one summer night, step outside or sit before a window.

Step 2: Look to the tallest tree in the darkening horizon. Breathe deep and sit or stand tall.

Step 3: Now gaze upon the tree's shadow, how far it reaches, and the different shapes that spring from it. See the grasses and any animals that rest in that massive shade.

Step 4: Think of your shadow and whom it touches. Visualize everything that has been affected by your shade.

Step 5: Build up your energy and let it surround you. Think of the shadows you stepped into. Those that were set before you began life and how you tried to match them.

Step 6: Once more, focus on the tree. See its great shelter and look to the sky. The darkness above is the great shadow. It hangs overhead for all of us to follow, to step into one day. Explore this thought and let it power your spirit on a journey.

Step 7: Meditate for as long as you can focus. When exhausted, sit back and breathe deeply. Rest.

26

TREE AGING
RITUALS

THE RITUAL OF LIFE CHANGES WITH US. As we grow, so too do our practices. No matter how advanced a person may be, they will always need ceremony and decorum.

The habits that carry us through life are most important in our later years. It is more challenging to meet expectations at times, but even more important to keep trying. Looking to the trees as honored friends and incorporating them into rituals gives new life to aging. This allows a positive gateway into the role of the "crone" or "wise woman."

Watching Leaves

(To be done in autumn for acceptance of mortality)

MATERIALS NEEDED: Leafy tree, basket, green candle, and matches

PREPARATION: Do in autumn once the leaves start to fall.

THE WORK:

1. Go before a tree and bow to its wisdom. Walk around it and collect leaves to fill the basket.

2. Find a comfortable space before the tree or nearby and place the basket before you. Take up the candle and chant, sing, or whisper of embracing the season's change and life changes.

3. Meditate on the candle and feel its warming energy. Build up your power.

4. Now take up the basket and place a hand onto the leaves. Meditate on each one's meaning and the beauty that resides in their fall.

5. Draw strength and calm from knowing that as the leaves crumble, they nourish the land for future hopes.

6. Sit back and enjoy the knowledge as the candle burns out. Ground yourself in your purpose, and thank the gods for all you are.

Swaying Through Limitations

(To increase flexibility)

MATERIALS NEEDED: Chair and glass of water
PREPARATION: Bless the water with healing energy.

THE WORK:

1. Sit before a window or on a patio/deck. Look to the trees and/or greenery before you.

2. Clear your mind. Breathe deep.

3. Now focus on new limitations and/or frustrations. Whether a new physical ailment or mental deficiencies due to stroke or other brain issues, lend your power to it. Give voice to every doubt and sensation that followed it.

4. Sit back. Take a sip of water. Be conscious of the liquid passing through you. Feel it cool the body.

5. Build your energies and visualize them as a healing light. Make it grow and direct it to the area that is most hindered.

6. Now look to the tree/plants and gently sway. Test the movement, and let it become more exaggerated with each repetition. Stay within your comfort zone.

7. As you sway, chant, sing, or whisper of caring for yourself as you are.

8. Once the energy is at its peak, stop. The body no longer heals or recovers like it used to. Embrace that and listen to what it has to tell you.

9. Take another drink of water and ground yourself in the love of your figure, no matter how it changes.

Embracing Bark

(To increase self-acceptance during aging)

MATERIALS NEEDED: A mirror and a tree
PREPARATION: Charge the mirror with your energies

THE WORK:

1. Sit or stand before a trusted tree (or look at one through a window/ in a picture). Breathe deep and clear your mind.

2. Focus on the beauty of the great giant. Turn the mirror toward it and chant, sing, or whisper of embracing aged beauty. Close your eyes and meditate on it.

3. Now look again. Turn the mirror facing yourself. Study the beauty of laugh lines, crinkles around the eyes, and a face that defies time. Chant, sing, or whisper of the changes you see and how they represent your life and the love you have known.

4. Close your eyes and meditate on appreciating your physical appearance. Visualize yourself in your youth, adulthood, middle age, and beyond.

5. When exhausted, open your eyes. Set the mirror down and look at the tree once more. Run your fingers over your face and smile. Thank the tree and ground yourself.

Growing into an Elder

(For building confidence to take on a greater role)

MATERIALS NEEDED: Picture or drawing of a trusted grand-parent or another elder (can be a figure from history you admire), tree or other plant, water or tea

PREPARATION: Charge the liquid with your energies

THE WORK:

1. Sit before the tree or plant with the picture to your right and the drink to your left.

2. Breathe deep and clear your mind. Look to the tree. Focus on the power, strength, and beauty it displays.

3. Look to the picture. Hold it. Study it. Recall (or visualize) the person behind the image: who they were, how they laughed and cried like everyone else.

4. Hold the picture up to the tree. Chant, sing, or whisper of their energy, how the trees and this elder aided your own personal growth.

5. Meditate on the qualities you admired on your journey and how they influenced you to become the person you are today.

6. Build your energies. Sit tall. Let the warmth inside you grow and grow until you cannot sit still. Now stand. Raise your arms up (if unable to stand, just look up). Chant, sing, and/or declare that you will be the elder you admire. Push the words forth and make them a reality.

7. Dedicate yourself to your new role, and thank the gods.

Rooting New Seeds

(To pass on your legacy to the younger generation)

MATERIALS NEEDED: Seeds or sapling, water, preferred cleans-ing herb, trusted young person/youthful family member

PREPARATION: Bless the water. Best done in springtime or summer.

THE WORK:

1. Sit across from the youth. Place the seeds between you and the water to your left, the preferred cleansing herb, and matches to your right.

2. Have the youth cleanse the space by burning your preferred cleansing herb and walking a circle around you both in each direction.

3. Then consecrate each other with the water by gently flicking it one at a time. Elder first, then youth. Chant, sing, or whisper of life and limb, how we are born to grow and carry what our roots hold with us.

4. Now have both of you place your hands over the seeds. Build your energies. Let them glow and warm you. Let them grow and extend down your arms and through your fingertips into the seeds.

5. Tell the youth: I pass these onto you, so they may grow as you do.

6. Have the youth reply: I take up these seeds to plant along my being.

7. Bow to each other and hug.

8. Laugh and sing and speak of life. Share ideas. Instruct the youth to plant the seeds within the current moon cycle.

Celebrating Tradition

(For appreciating milestones and the passage of time)

MATERIALS NEEDED: Pictures, mementos, family heirlooms, and close family members

PREPARATION: Best done during a special holiday or birthday

celebration.

THE WORK:

1. Have everyone place their items on a large table or altar. Mix and mingle, just talk and share the company, the atmosphere.

2. When everyone is settled in, turn to the altar and get comfortable. Have everyone meditate together, focusing on your connections that build trust and love.

3. Now stand and lead a chant/prayer of honoring your traditions and what they mean to everyone there.

4. Bow to each other and continue enjoying the moments you share.

Looking to the Clouds

(To find new endeavors)

MATERIALS NEEDED: Yourself, a tree, and a seedy dandelion (if none can be found, use a flower with petals)

PREPARATION: Must be done on a cloudy day. Best performed during a waxing moon cycle, during light hours.

THE WORK:

1. Sit outside or before an open window (no screen).

2. Hold the dandelion and gaze at the clouds. Look to the tree reaching into the vapors, working on testing new limits. Meditate on that resilience, that drive to go on, no matter how age may affect your being.

3. Think of what hobbies and interests you've enjoyed in life.

4. Now recall those endeavors you wished to fulfill that have remained

untouched. If they no longer interest you, open your senses and seek out a new idea to follow. Something you can do that would make your days more agreeable. Focus on the easier ones, the most realistic ways to "reach further."

5. Build your energy. Let it warm you and glow. Push it into the dandelion or flower.

6. Chant, sing, or whisper a dedication to making this new idea a reality. See yourself taking up a new hobby or achievement.

7. Blow the dandelion seeds into the sky, pluck the flower petals, and toss them to the wind. Watch the dance of nature before you. Trust in the energies that flower between us all.

8. Bow to the tree and the sky. Thank the gods, and prepare to begin your new activity.

Sharing Strength

(To offer spiritual strength to others)

MATERIALS NEEDED: A stick and 2 candles (1 white, 1 black)
PREPARATION: Charge the candles with your energy.

THE WORK:

1. Place the candles in the center of your altar or workspace and set the stick in front of them.

2. Meditate on the stick, focusing on its hard form.

3. Think of yourself and your inner strength, where it comes from and how you use it. Build your energies and feel them warming you, illuminating your being.

4. Light the black candle and sing, chant, or whisper to draw forth that

personal power. Let it multiply and fill the space.

5. Light the white candle and sing, chant, or whisper to send your power into the world. Visualize others being charged with balance and purpose. See them alive and free.

6. Then sit back and ground yourself. Bow to the stick, burn it in the next fire or keep it as an altar gift.

Pruning Your Power

(To end bad habits later in life)

MATERIALS NEEDED: Water, preferred cleansing herb and matches, trusted tree or houseplant, pruning shears
PREPARATION: Bless the water. Best done during the waning moon cycle.

THE WORK:

1. Place the shears before the tree or houseplant.

2. Cleanse the space by burning the cleansing herb.

3. Now sit and meditate on the plant. Pour half of the water on the roots and chant, sing, or whisper of its living energy, the connection you hold with it.

4. Shift your focus to yourself. Meditate on your core elements. What makes you bloom and blossom like a great elder tree.

5. Take up the pruning shears and think of the faults that have followed you throughout your life. Turn to the tree and seek out weak branches or leaves. Cut them back as needed. Visualize your faults being pruned as you do this.

6. Rest and think of the newer issues that have come into your life and begun draining your power, aspects of your own being that are hindering your balance. Once more, turn to the tree and look more carefully. Weed out weak buds or branches, and trim and shape the plant or tree while seeking to prune your own.

7. When finished, bow to the tree. Then breathe deeply and drink the rest of the water.

27

TREE AGING
SPELLS

THERE ARE NO ANTI-AGING SPELLS HERE. AGE IS a gift that reveals our true beauty. It allows us to become the teachers we love, to mold young minds, and step into the future with light and laughter.

Tree spellwork eases transitions. It offers truth and courage rooted in nature. When looking at the reality of death from a closer standpoint, the magic within holds the potential to extend its roots and prepare us for the shift of balance and power that lies ahead. Unleashing that magic is eternal.

Finding your Sheltering Spirit

MATERIALS NEEDED: Salt, water, preferred cleansing herb and matches, Rhodochrosite stone, and athame

PREPARATION: Bless the water and charge the stone with your energy. Set your altar or space with the stone in the center, the salt to the east, the water to the water, the preferred cleansing herb and matches to the south, and the athame to the north.

THE WORK:

1. Cast a circle before an open window or familiar tree with the salt and water, then cleanse the space with the cleansing herb.

2. Raise your arms before the stone and call upon the power of the Gods by the grace of the trees surrounding your area. Build your energies. Feel the power warm you and visualize its illumination.

3. Take up the athame and point it to the trees. Chant, sing, or whisper of drawing from the tree's protective shade.

4. Touch the point to the stone and chant, sing, or whisper to draw out the stone's compassion.

5. Now point the blade above you and chant, sing, or whisper for the universe to aid you on your journey through old age. Ask to spread your protective energy, but to never become overly guarded. Ask to be humbled and enlightened, wise but never without laughter. Ask to be whole as a being so you can better prepare for what comes after.

6. Replace the athame and take up the stone. Sit and meditate on your power and its meaning.

7. When exhausted, break the circle and ground yourself.

Seeking Trust in the Trees

(To heighten intuition)

MATERIALS NEEDED: Salt, water, preferred cleansing herb and matches, moonstone, wooded area, or houseplant

PREPARATION: Bless the water and charge the stone. Set your altar or workspace with the stone at the foot of a friendly tree or houseplant. Place the preferred cleansing herb before it, the water before the preferred cleansing herb, and the salt before the water in a perfect line.

THE WORK:

1. Cast a circle with the salt and water. Then take up the preferred cleansing herb and wave it over your body, then the tree, before cleansing the entire space.

2. Now take up the moonstone in one hand and place your other palm on the tree or plant. This can be done standing, sitting, or however is most comfortable.

3. Chant, sing, or whisper of trust and truth in the trees.

4. Build your energies as you chant. Repeat the words again and again. If compelled to rock and sway, do so.

5. As the warmth flows through you, visualize its illumination. See the stone shine.

6. Now look to the tree and dedicate yourself to its knowledge and honesty. Ask for insight and the ability to serve as a communicator.

7. Be open to the unwavering realities that may surface. Be willing to take on all you can bear. Be ready to teach and meet your end with grace and dignity.

8. Now relax. Breathe deep. Press the stone to your forehead and blow the tree a kiss.

Connecting Vines Spell

(To increase personal power)

MATERIALS NEEDED: Salt, water, preferred cleansing herb and matches, rhodochrosite stone, green ribbon, vine from tree or plant (English Ivy works best, be careful to avoid poison ivy, etc.)

PREPARATION: Bless the water and charge the stone with your energies. Set the ribbon out in the moonlight during a full moon. Set your altar with the stone and ribbon in the center, the vine to the north, the preferred cleansing herb and matches to the south, the salt to the east, and the water to the west.

THE WORK:

1. Cast a circle with the salt and water. Cleanse the space with the preferred cleansing herb.

2. Now take up the vine. Hold it close to you and meditate on its ability to stretch on and on, how it lives with vigor and progress.

3. Set the vine before the stone and hold the rhodochrosite in your hands. Feel its power and purpose. Build your energies with it.

4. Keep the stone in your left and hold your right over the vine. Chant, sing, or whisper of connecting the climbing nature of the vine with your path to let your spirit reach higher levels.

5. Now take up the ribbon. Wrap it around the vine to contain the meaning while aiding it. Meditate on growing like the vine yet remaining in control like the ribbon.

6. When fully wrapped, bow to the vine. Thank it and the universe for your continued journey.

7. Break the circle and ground yourself.

Learning to Teach

(To pass on energies and spiritual practices)

MATERIALS NEEDED: Salt, water, preferred cleansing herb and matches, Moonstone, paper and pen

PREPARATION: Bless the water, charge the stone, and meditate on the blank paper. Set your altar with the pen and paper at the center, the stone to the north, the preferred cleansing herb and matches to the south, the salt to the east, and the water to the west.

THE WORK:

1. Cast a circle with the salt and water. Cleanse the space with the preferred cleansing herb.

2. Now sit before the pen and paper. Take up the moonstone. Feel its energy. Draw that power into you. Let it flow throughout your mind and out your fingertips.

3. Grab the pen and draw a large tree with many branches (drawing skills are not necessary. Even stick figures work).

4. Now focus on the tree as a symbol of wisdom. Hold the pen in your dominant hand and the stone in the other. Chant, sing, or whisper of becoming a source of knowledge, discovering the many ways to teach and breakthrough.

5. Write how you wish to teach others on each branch. Let ideas and thoughts bud and grow. Keep writing until the tree is filled or your mind becomes exhausted.

6. Fold the paper and place the moonstone on top of it. Set the pen down and hold the paper and stone together. Ask the Gods to aid you on this quest to educate.

7. Meditate on any experience you've had passing on ideas to others. Let that power build and solidify.

8. Then sit back and relax. Breathe deep. Break the circle and ground yourself in your role.

Digging up Truth

(For increased intuition)

MATERIALS NEEDED: Salt, water, preferred cleansing herb and matches, Lapis Lazuli stone, athame, trusted tree or houseplant

PREPARATION: Bless the water and charge the stone with your energies. Leave the athame out on a full moon to absorb the lunar power. Place the stone before the tree or houseplant. Set the athame to the north, the preferred cleansing herb and matches to the south, the water to the west, and salt to the east.

THE WORK:

1. Cast a circle using salt and water. Cleanse the space with the preferred cleansing herb.

2. Grab the stone and hold it up to the tree. Sing, chant, or whisper for intuition and ideas rooted in truth.

3. Meditate on the stone and feel its power. Extend your energies and link them to it.

4. Set it back down and take up the athame. Hold it up and draw down the lunar power into yourself.

5. Point the blade at the tree and sing, chant, or whisper of binding honesty to your purpose.

6. Use the athame to dig in the soil. Bury the stone before the tree or in the houseplant pot and cover it.

7. Hold your hands over the spot. Feel your connection and let it grow.

8. Sit back and relax. Welcome what thoughts come to you. Break the circle and ground yourself.

9. After the next moon cycle, dig up the stone and let it guide you through future meditations and rituals.

Spell for Courage

(To bravely face the future)

MATERIALS NEEDED: WSalt, water, preferred cleansing herb, and matches, rose quartz, mirror, trusted tree or houseplant

PREPARATION: Bless the salt and charge the stone with your energy. Set your altar or workspace before the plant with the stone on the mirror. Put the preferred cleansing herb and matches directly in front of the mirror, then the water in front of the cleansing herb, and the salt in front of the water in a straight line.

THE WORK:

1. Cast a circle with the salt and water, then cleanse the space with the cleansing herb.

2. Sit before the plant and meditate on its rough outer bark.

3. Take up the stone and feel its energy. Draw that hopeful power into yourself. For hope breeds courage.

4. Hold the stone in one hand and grab the mirror with the other. Look at your reflection and display the stone in your image. Chant, sing, or whisper of your hope.

5. Turn the mirror to face the tree. Chant, sing, or whisper to take heed from the wise giant.

6. Replace the mirror before the tree and set the stone on it again. Reach up high and dedicate yourself to honoring yourself and your values no matter what happens.

7. Bow to the tree.

8. Take up the stone and the mirror one last time. Smile at yourself and tell your image that you will not fall prey to fear.

9. Bind it with a kiss.

10. Relax. Break the circle and ground yourself.

Balancing the Future

(To be done during a full moon and accept the unknown)

MATERIALS NEEDED: Salt, water, preferred cleansing herb and matches, White Jade stone, 2 candles (1 black and 1 white), tree or houseplant

PREPARATION: Bless the water and charge the stone with your energies. Set the preferred cleansing herb and matches at the south end of the altar, the water to the west, the salt to the east, and the stone to the north, with the candle in the center. This is best performed on a full moon.

THE WORK:

1. Cast a circle with the salt and water, then cleanse the space with the cleansing herb.

2. Call upon the powers of the elements to bring balance and order, to help guide you into a better future.

3. Light the candles, first the black, then the white, and chant for the darkness and the light to mingle with perfect harmony.

4. Take up the stone and feel its power surge. Draw it into you.

5. Gaze up and ask the universe to help you bless the unknown, to walk with you through uncertainty, and guide you into the great beyond.

6. Follow whatever you may.

7. When exhausted, rest and break the circle. Ground yourself and replenish your energies with a feast.

Transferring Power Spell

(End of life farewell)

MATERIALS NEEDED: Salt, water, preferred cleansing herb and matches, jade stone, athame, a cup of wine or water (for drinking), wooded area or houseplant, trusted youth

PREPARATION: Perform when ready to pass on but still energetic enough to complete. You will know when. Bless the water. Set up your altar or workspace before the plant. Set the drinking cup in front of it with the athame centered so the stone sits at the north, the salt at the east, the water at the west, and the preferred cleansing herb and matches to the south.

THE WORK:

1. Cast a circle with the salt and water. Cleanse the space with the cleansing herb.

2. Call upon the elements.

3. Bow before the tree or plant together. Hold hands and dedicate yourself to the power of life and death.

4. Hold the stone in between your hands and push your energies into it. Chant, sing, or whisper of offering your power to this young person. Hand the stone off to them.

5. They must now chant, sing, or whisper of accepting this power to aid with balance and knowledge in the future.

6. Now take up the athame. Hold it up to the sky and call upon the Gods to consecrate this great work.

7. Point the blade at the tree and say: By the power of the roots that bind us all, so mote it be!

8. Point the blade at the youth and have them repeat this line: By the power of the roots that bind us all, so mote it be!

9. Hand over the athame.

10. Bow to each other and kiss on the cheek. Break the circle.

11. Your power will not be gone but less intense. Your will and ways will carry you more than the magic that once led.

Magic for All

(To send your spiritual understanding out into the world)

MATERIALS NEEDED: Salt, water, preferred cleansing herb and matches, diamond, globe, crystal ball, 2 white candles, tree or houseplant

PREPARATION: Bless the water. Place the crystal ball before the plant. Set the diamond at the north, the salt to the east, the water to the west, the cleansing herb and matches to the south, and the candles (one on either side of the globe at the center).

THE WORK:

1. Cast a circle with the salt and water, then cleanse the space with the preferred cleansing herb.

2. Call upon the elements from the four corners of the earth.

3. Light the candles and chant, sing, or whisper for the Gods to light the way for humanity.

4. Close your eyes and meditate on the globe. Visualize the balancing energy of magic in everyone. See it powering life and death, light and dark, in perfect harmony with love and trust.

5. Look at the crystal ball. Rub your fingertips over it. Chant, sing, or whisper to see the will of the future. Study it, be open and ready to receive all understanding.

6. Take up the diamond and feel its incredible power. Hold it before the crystal ball and the globe. Now speak with vigor: By the power of three times three, I send true magic awareness unto thee!

7. Repeat this three times, pushing out all your energy.

8. Now sit back. Breathe deep. Know that as your time fades, so shall a new era dawn. Accept your fate and smile at passing something on.

9. Break the circle and ground yourself. Blessed be.

CONCLUSION: CONTINUE TO GROW

TREE ENERGIES ARE WITH US, MUCH LIKE OUR creators, even when we can't see them. Our bond with other living beings is consecrated with the soil and roots that hold the earth together. I hope I properly conveyed that in this book. Whether you utilize every chapter, or just a few meditations, the natural magic is within us all. From the first moment of our lives, the trees are there. Many will remain standing long after we're gone.

I wrote this book during the 2020 COVID-19 pandemic. Through-out those early lockdowns, the forests were still there for me. Parks and trails remained to be explored. Birds still sang, and the animals continued their cycle of life and death without change.

The trees in my backyard remained friends. No matter how closed-off the world became, the sky was still blue, and the trees continued to paint it with emerald and gold leaves. My great love for the wooden giants allowed my family and me to laugh and live without fear.

No matter what happens in the future, I wish that for everyone. Having lived in the city, the suburbs, and played in the country, I want everyone to know that nothing can prevent them from growing and maturing as needed. When you feel stunted, look to the trees. No matter how small or aged, there is life in the roots, energy. Power.

Trees never stop growing, not until they are dead. That's something we can all aspire to do. Go and grow with love.

AUTHOR

Jessica Marie Baumgartner

Jessica is a Pagan mother of four, whose children's books about love and understanding have received critical acclaim and multiple awards. She is a member of the Missouri Writer's Guild and author of "The Magic of Nature: Meditations and Spells to Find Your Inner Voice," "Walk Your Path," "The Golden Rule," and "My Family Is Different." Her work has been featured by, "Witch Way Magazine," "Witchology Magazine," "Aspire Magazine," "Light of Consciousness Magazine," "Conscious Shift Magazine," "The New Spirit Journal," "Chicken Soup for the Soul," "Circle Magazine," "The Witches' Voice," and many more.

WORKS CITED

Ackerman S. "Discovering the Brain." National Academies Press. 1992. Print & Web. https://www.ncbi.nlm.nih.gov/books/NBK234146/

Brean, Joseph. "Seeing faces in trees correlates to creativity, and cognitive scientists are taking interest." National Post. 28 Feb, 2020. Web. https://nationalpost.com/news/seeing-faces-in-trees-correlates-to-creativity-and-cognitive-scientists-are-taking-interest

Flemming, Nic. "Plants talk to each-other using and internet of fungus." BBC Earth. 11th Nov, 2014. Web. http://www.bbc.com/earth/story/20141111-plants-have-a-hidden-internet

Goldbaum, Kate. "What is the Oldest Tree in the World." Live Science. 23, Aug. 2016. Web. https://www.livescience.com/29152-oldest-tree-in-world.html

Grant, Richard. "Do Trees Talk to Each Other?" Smithsonian Magazine. March 2018. Web. https://www.smithsonianmag.com/science-nature/the-whispering-trees-180968084/

Guiness World Records. "Oldest Living Individual Tree." 27th, Jan, 2020. Web. https://www.guinnessworldrecords.com/world-records/oldest-living-individual-tree

IRS Notice. "Tax Deductions for Commercial Buildings." Energy Star. Jan, 2020. Web. https://www.energystar.gov/about/federal_tax_credits/federal_tax_credit_archive/tax_credits_commercial_buildings

Kardan, O., Gozdyra, P., Misic, B. et al. "Neighborhood greenspace and health in a large urban center." Sci Rep 5, 11610. 9 July, 2015. https://doi.org/10.1038/srep11610

Long, Ben. "Urban trees found to improve mental and general health." University of Wollongong. 26, July 2019. Web. https://phys.org/news/2019-07-urban-trees-mental-health.html

McTaggart, Lynne. "The Intention Experiment: Using Your Thoughts to Change Your Life and the World." Free Press. 9th Jan, 2007. Print.

Missouri Department of Conservation. "Rockwoods Reservation." 3rd Aug, 2020. Web. https://nature.mdc.mo.gov/discover-nature/places/rockwoods-reservation

Office of Energy Efficiency & Renewable Energy. "A National Network of Local Coalitions." Department of Energy. 2020. Web. https://cleancities.energy.gov/coalitions/

"One Trillion Trees Achievements." 1 Trillion Trees. 3rd, Aug 2020. Web. http://1trilliontrees.org/

Rasputin, Maria, Barham, Patte. "Rasputin: the Man Behind the Myth." Warner Books. 1st Jun, 1978. Print.

Urban Institute. "Baby's Brain Begins Now: Conception to Age 3." 28th Jan, 2020. Web. http://www.urbanchildinstitute.org/why-0-3/baby-and-brain

Zarlenga, Dan. "Rockwoods Reservation Celebrates 75 Years As Missouri's First Conservation Area." MO Department of Conservation. 12th June, 2020. Web. https://mdc.mo.gov/newsroom/rockwoods-reservation-celebrates-75-years-missouri-s-first-conservation-area

Zerbe, Dean. "The Green Tax Breaks for Architects, Engineers, And Contractors: Section 179D Update. Forbes. 27th July 2020, Web. https://www.forbes.com/sites/deanzerbe/2020/07/27/the-green-tax-break-for-architects-engineers-and-contractors-section-179d-update/#42055dac7c6f

Zimmerman, Kim Anne. "Pareidolia: Seeing Faces in Unusual Places." Live Science. 11 Dec, 2012. Web. https://www.livescience.com/25448-pareidolia.html

Zarlenga, Dan. "Rockwoods Reservation Celebrates 75 Years As Missouri's First Conservation Area." MO Department of Conservation. 12th June, 2020. Web. https://mdc.mo.gov/newsroom/rockwoods-reservation-celebrates-75-years-missouri-s-first-conservation-area

CPSIA information can be obtained
at www.ICGtesting.com
Printed in the USA
LVHW081230140223
739386LV00012B/184